WORLD WAR II

JON & DIANE SUTHERLAND

FLAME TREE
PUBLISHING

CONTENTS

Many factors were involved in the lead-up to the war, not least Germany's treatment at the hands of World War I's victors – the territorial, military and financial restrictions and reparations forced upon Germany by the 1919 Treaty of Versailles. This section considers the causes and context of the path to war.

After cementing relations with Italy and Russia, Germany was ready to act on its territorial designs: **1 SEPT** – Germany invades Poland ➤ **3 SEPT** – Britain and France declare war on Germany ➤ **5 SEPT** – German troops cross the Vistula River ➤ **17 SEPT** – The Soviet Union invades Poland; HMS *Courageous* is sunk ➤ **27 SEPT** – Warsaw falls to the Germans ➤ **14 OCT** – HMS *Royal Oak* is sunk by a German U-boat ➤ **8 NOV** – The Munich Plot ➤ **13 DEC** – The Battle of the River Plate begins ➤ **28 DEC** – Rationing introduced in Britain.

Germany pushes on: **9 APR** – Germany invades Norway ➤ **10 MAY** – Chamberlain resigns and Churchill takes over; Germany invades Belgium and Holland ➤ **15 MAY** – Holland surrenders ➤ **27 MAY** – Evacuation of Dunkirk begins ➤ **28 MAY** – Belgium surrenders ➤ **5 JUNE** – The Battle of France begins ➤ **10 JUNE** – Italy declares war ➤ **14 JUNE** – The Germans enter Paris; Italy invades France ➤ **17 JUNE** – The Soviet Union invades the Baltic States ➤ **28 JUNE** – De Gaulle becomes leader of the Free French ➤ **4 AUG** – War begins in East Africa ➤ **8 AUG** – The Battle of Britain begins ➤ **7 SEPT** – The Blitz begins ➤ **27 SEPT** – Germany, Italy and Japan sign the Tripartite Pact ➤ **7 OCT** – German troops invade Romania ➤ **20 NOV** – Hungary enters the war ➤ **9 DEC** – Britain launches North African offensive.

1941 60

Further countries are drawn into the war's web: **5 JAN** – Allied forces enter Libya » **1 MAR** – Auschwitz-Brikenau opens » **30 MAR** – The Germans launch an offensive in North Africa » **6 APR** – Germany invades Yugoslavia » **13 APR** – Russia and Japan sign a non-aggression treaty » **17 APR** – Yugoslavia surrenders to the Germans; Britain launches an offensive in Iraq » **21 APR** – Greece surrenders to the Germans » **6 MAY** – Stalin becomes Soviet Premier » **22 JUNE** – Germany invades the Soviet Union » **14 JULY** – British troops occupy Syria » **31 JULY** – Goering presents the Final Solution » **8 SEPT** – The Siege of Leningrad begins » **7 DEC** – Japan attacks Pearl Harbor » **8 DEC** – The Allies declare war on Japan » **11 DEC** – Germany and Italy declare war on the US » **25 DEC** – The Japanese capture Hong Kong.

1942 102

Japan is relentless in its pursuit of territory: **2 JAN** – The Japanese capture Manila » **16 JAN** – The Japanese attack Burma » **15 FEB** – Singapore falls to the Japanese » **7 MAR** – Java falls to the Japanese » **8 MAR** – The Japanese take Rangoon » **28 MAR** – Allied forces attack St Nazaire » **9 APR** – The Japanese capture Bataan » **18 APR** – The Dolittle air raid against Tokyo is launched » **4 MAY** – The Battle of the Coral Sea begins » **5 MAY** – Operation Ironclad begins » **30 MAY** – The thousand-bomber raid is launched » **4 JUNE** – The Battle of Midway begins » **1 JULY** – The Germans capture Sevastopol » **26 JULY** – The RAF begins raids on Hamburg » **7 AUG** – US marines land on Guadalcanal » **19 AUG** – The Allies raid Dieppe » **30 AUG** – The First Battle of El Alamein begins » **15 SEPT** – The Battle of Stalingrad begins » **8 NOV** – Operation Torch is initiated.

T33417

The Allies make progress as the war grinds on: **14 JAN** – The Casablanca Conference opens » **18 JAN** – Leningrad is liberated » **3 MAR** – The Battle of Bismarck Sea begins » **18 MAR** – The US shoots down Yamamoto » **7 MAY** – Tunis falls to the Allies » **16 MAY** – The Dambuster raids » **5 JULY** – The Germans launch Operation Citadel » **10 JULY** – The Allies begin their European invasions » **17 JULY** – The battle for Bougainville commences » **25 JULY** – Mussolini is imprisoned » **1 AUG** – Operation Tidalwave is launched by the Allies » **17 AUG** – The US wins the race for Messina » **8 SEPT** – Italy surrenders » **10 SEPT** – The Germans capture Rome » **13 SEPT** – The Germans massacre Greeks on Cephalonia » **13 OCT** – Italy declares war on Germany » **6 NOV** – Kiev is liberated.

The Allies regain ground in the year of the D-Day landings: **30 JAN** – The Allies land on the Marshall Islands » **6 FEB** – The Battle of the Dniepr begins » **3 APR** – Operation Tungsten is launched » **9 MAY** – Sevastopol is liberated » **4 JUNE** – Rome falls to the Allies » **6 JUNE** – Operation Overlord begins with the D-Day landings » **8 JUNE** – The Soviets launch an offensive against Finland » **15 JUNE** – First US bombing raid against Japan » **9 JULY** – Saipan falls to the US » **21 JULY** – US marines land at Guam » **24 JULY** – The Soviets liberate Majdanek concentration camp » **25 JULY** – Operation Cobra begins » **4 AUG** – Anne Frank and her family are arrested » **15 AUG** – Paris is liberated by the Allies » **17 SEPT** – Operation Market Garden is launched » **18 OCT** – The Soviets push into Prussia » **29 NOV** – Albania is liberated by the Allies.

The war eventually draws to a close but not before the detonation of a devastating weapon: **17 JAN** – The Soviets capture Warsaw » **3 FEB** – Manila is liberated by US troops » **7 MAR** – The Allies take the bridge at Remagen » **9 MAR** – Air raids are launched over Tokyo » **5 APR** – The Japanese government collapses » **11 APR** – The Allies liberate Buchenwald » **13 APR** – The Soviets capture Vienna » **28 APR** – Mussolini is assassinated » **30 APR** – Hitler commits suicide » **1 MAY** – Berlin falls to the Allies » **4 MAY** – The Germans accept an unconditional surrender » **22 MAY** – The British capture Himmler » **6 AUG** – The atomic bomb is dropped on Hiroshima » **14 AUG** – Japan accepts an unconditional surrender » **2 SEPT** – VJ day is celebrated » **20 NOV** – The Nuremberg trials begin.

From ill-fated Chamberlain to people's hero Churchill, from chilling Himmler to passionate dictator Mussolini, the key protagonists and antagonists of the war are all covered here in succinct entries organized in alphabetical order.

The end of the war may have brought peace but the world was far from trouble-free; the countries involved had lost power, empires had suffered and diminished, states were left physically damaged and financially ruined. Seeds were sown that arguably contributed to later conflicts, as far ahead as today's ongoing Middle Eastern unrest. This section is a thoughtful discussion of the war's enduring legacy.

INTRODUCTION

The importance of the subject of this book can scarcely be over-emphasized. Unparalleled in scale by any other conflict in human history, World War II is generally estimated to have cost the lives of 50 million people. In terms of human suffering its effects are incalculable, and the physical destruction that it wrought took decades to repair. Without a full knowledge of this cataclysmic event it is impossible to understand fully the history of the second half of the twentieth century.

New Super Powers

This was the war that propelled the USA to the status of 'Super-Power', by hugely enhancing its economy and military might. Another of the war's victors, the Soviet Union, matched American power for over 40 years, creating the Cold War. That a real war never erupted between these antagonists was largely due to the fact that both possessed arsenals of nuclear weapons – another development of World War II. Meanwhile, with their economies shattered by the war, the traditional 'Great Powers' of western and central Europe lost much of their influence in the world. They also proved unable, through lack of economic power and political will, to hold onto their empires.

Middle East & Asia

In the Middle East, the creation of the state of Israel was hastened by the arrival of Jewish survivors of Nazi persecution. Israel's aggressive defence of its independence, against attempts by neighbouring Arab states to extinguish it, resulted in recurring conflicts during the second half of the twentieth century. Its existence remains the central factor in the complicated politics of the region. Further east, China, already ravaged by civil wars, had been invaded by Japan in 1937. By 1945 its Nationalist government was so weakened and discredited that Mao Tse Tung's well-organized army was able to begin the unification of the world's largest nation under Communist rule.

A meeting of the Allied leaders during World War II.

A Global War

The war itself exhibited many novel features. Firstly it was a global war: few regions of the world remained untouched by its effects. Furthermore, civilian populations experienced war on a wider scale than ever before. Even those fortunate enough to escape invasion, bombardment, enemy occupation or famine could be affected by the unprecedented level of mobilization on the home front or, at the very least, by shortages caused by the disruption of international trade.

Preparations for the First Battle of El Alamein in 1942.

World War II was also a war of conflicting political ideologies. This conflict was complicated by the fact that western democracies were obliged to make a common cause against Nazism, Fascism and Japanese Militarism with the Communist Soviet Union. The western Allies had no territorial claims to make on their opponents; their sole aim was to destroy the enemy political regimes. The USSR had very real ambitions to expand its power, but was happy to achieve this by imposing the rule of Soviet-controlled Communist governments in countries that Soviet troops had liberated.

Weaponry

Many of the weapons and tactics employed in World War II originated in World War I; however, the technological advances of the intervening 20 years now allowed them to show

their full devastating potential. The early German successes were built on their so-called Blitzkrieg tactics – employing massed tanks with close air support. As the war progressed, these tactics were refined and adopted by other countries too – most successfully by the USSR. Change was equally evident in naval warfare, where the rise to prominence of naval aviation ensured that the aircraft carrier replaced the battleship as the prime naval unit. Meanwhile ocean-going submarines fought major campaigns in the Atlantic and Pacific Oceans. Massed aerial bombing of enemy cities was pioneered by the Germans, but brought to a terrifying peak of efficiency by the British and Americans against Germany, and the Americans against Japan. The latter campaign culminated in the deployment of a wholly new type of weapon – the atomic bomb.

Concise Account

All these aspects of World War II are clearly and concisely presented to the reader of this book. Descriptions of the events and campaigns appear in chronological order, along with the political background from which they sprang. Interspersed within this structure are discussions of the tactics and weapons used. The book is further enlivened by the inclusion of biographies of the leading political and military figures of the era. Full advantage is taken of the ready availability of memorable photographs of the conflict.

In happy contrast with many previous publications on the subject, the huge Soviet contribution to the defeat of Germany is given due weight in this book. There is full coverage of the colossal battles of the Eastern Front, which did more than anything else to destroy the fighting power of the German army. Finally, that uniquely appalling aspect of World War II, the Holocaust, is dealt with as an integrated part of the whole. This is just as it should be, as the Holocaust is inextricably bound up with the war itself. It was a war within a war, and, horrifically, was regarded as a completely valid form of military 'duty' by many of its perpetrators. The Holocaust could not have been carried out outside the context of World War II, and its memory remains the grimmest legacy of that terrible conflict.

Paul Cornish

THE CAUSES OF WAR

PRECURSORS TO CONFLICT

Historians are unable to agree as the causes of World War II. The conflict was not a question of personal ambition, nor a desire for power. There were deeper reasons which can be traced back at least to the settlement forced upon Germany under the terms of the 1919 Treaty of Versailles. The Japanese needed to extend their sphere of influence and access to resources beyond the islands which had constrained them for centuries.

Nationalistic Tensions

The punitive damages meted out on Germany as the belligerent power during World War I had caused domestic unrest in Germany. By the 1930s the two most powerful members of the League of Nations, Britain and France, were unwilling to back decisions with shows of force.

Bound By Treaties

Prior to Adolf Hitler's rise to power Germany had signed the Locarno Treaties in 1925. They had to accept the borders laid down in the Treaty of Versailles and agreed never to attack France or Belgium again. Germany also accepted that the Rhineland should remain a demilitarized zone. The associated treaties bound France to protect the territorial integrity of Belgium, Czechoslovakia and Poland; due to Britain's treaties with France, this meant that Britain, too, was guaranteeing their integrity. The Kellogg-Briand Pact was signed in 1928, heralding an era of peace as the 65 signatory countries agreed to refrain from war.

Japanese Expansionism

From 1931 the Japanese were involved in attempts to conquer Manchuria. Manchuria's

200,000 sq km (77,000 sq miles) would provide the teeming Japanese population with an area of natural growth and settlement. The League of Nations, despite Chinese pleas, did not censure the Japanese.

The statue commemorating the establishment of the League of Nations.

Italian Expansionism

Between 1935 and 1936, in a desire to create a new African empire for Rome, Benito Mussolini had invaded Abyssinia and made the first use of mustard gas. Mussolini united Abyssinia, Eritrea and Somaliland and named the area Italian East Africa. Although the League of Nations condemned the Italians, little was done to prevent the incursion.

German Aggression

In direct opposition to the terms of the Treaty of Versailles, from 1935 Hitler began to rearm Germany by trebling the size of the army and ordering the construction of aircraft. He pushed the boundaries of the Treaty of Versailles and the patience of the League of Nations, yet Britain and France did not intervene.

Rhineland Crisis

The 1936 Rhineland crisis could have brought Britain and France's wrath upon Germany before Hitler was in a position to defend himself. Against strict international agreements, Hitler entered the demilitarized zone with 32,000 men.

Annexation of Austria

In 1938 the boundaries were pushed again when the question of Austria arose. Hitler considered Austria to be part of Germany, but he knew war would result if he simply marched in and seized the country. Instead he ensured that Arthur Seyss-Inquart, a prominent Austrian Nazi, obtained a senior government position. He then told the Austrian government that they should offer their citizens a referendum on possible unification with Germany. Hitler said that if the referendum was not agreed, then Austrian Chancellor Kurt von Schuschnigg should resign. If Schuschnigg did not choose one of these options then Hitler threatened to invade. Schuschnigg chose to resign, and his cabinet walked out in support. Only Seyss-Inquart remained and, as the only representative of the government left, he invited Hitler to cross the border.

Hitler's Nazi army.

Czechoslovakia

There was then the question of Czechoslovakia, created in the aftermath of World War I, containing 3.2 million Germans. The Germans lived in the Sudetenland region of the country and wanted to become part of Germany. The Czech government would not agree and Hitler proposed an invasion. Although France had guaranteed Czechoslovakia's territorial integrity, it seemed unlikely that the country would actually move against Germany.

Trying to Avoid War

Britain wished to avoid war after witnessing the Spanish Civil War from 1936.

Neville Chamberlain

In British Prime Minister Neville Chamberlain Hitler found a man who was wedded to peace. He used this to his advantage and convinced Chamberlain to sign over all parts of

Czechoslovakia that had a significant German-speaking population. A deal was concluded between Germany, Britain, France and Italy without negotiating with the Czechs and on 1 October 1938 Germany occupied Sudetenland.

Invading Czechoslovakia

Hitler was not content; he wanted Moravia and Bohemia as well, claiming that the Czechs were ill-treating the 500,000 German speakers in these regions. He said that if the German army was not invited across the border to restore law and order then he would have no choice but to bomb Prague. The Czech government caved in and on 15 March 1939 German troops marched into Prague; on the following day Bohemia and Moravia were made protectorates of Germany. All that remained was for Hitler to address the apparent plight of the Germans who now lived within the Polish borders.

Pact of Steel

Hitler began by cementing his relationships with vital European allies. Italy signed the Pact of Steel with Germany and in August 1939 the final piece in the jigsaw fell into place when the German Foreign Minister Joachim von Ribbentrop and the Russian Premier Vyachelsav Molotov signed the German-Russian Pact, which decreed that the two countries would not wage war against each other for a decade. Unknown to all at the time, a clause was included in the Pact which agreed that should either Germany or Russia attack Poland, then the country would be split between them. When Germany finally made that attack on 1 September 1939, the countries of Europe were past the point of compromise and with great reluctance, two days after Poland was invaded, Britain and France declared war on Germany.

Axis leaders Benito Mussolini and Adolf Hitler.

1939

SEPTEMBER

As German forces attacked Poland across all frontiers and its planes bombed Polish cities, including the capital, Warsaw, Britain and France declared war. Following the declaration, Britain experienced the Phoney War, while the Royal Navy suffered its first loss, HMS *Courageous*, to German U-boats.

1 September: Germany Invades Poland

Without a formal declaration of war, at 04:45, 53 German divisions began crossing the Polish border. Within a few hours Polish defences had been breached and as German aircraft pounded Polish cities, German tanks penetrated deep into Polish territory. As soon as the invasion became known, France and Britain demanded Germany's immediate withdrawal. By 2 September, German units had penetrated up to 80 km (50 miles). Polish resistance was shambolic and instantly broken up by German air attacks.

German troops enter Polish territory.

Italy Declares its Neutrality

The day after Germany's invasion, Italy declared itself neutral. On the same day the Germans announced they would not attack Norway provided Germany was not attacked by other countries; the Commonwealth responded by declaring war on Germany. On 4 September Japan declared its neutrality, and the USA followed suit the next day.

➧ see US Passes the Selective Service Act p. 52

3 September: Britain and France Declare War

At 09:00 on 3 September Britain delivered an ultimatum to Germany stating that unless it made undertakings to withdraw from Poland by 11:00 that day Britain would consider itself at war. At 12:00 the French delivered a similar ultimatum, set to expire the following day. Hitler had been convinced that the western powers would remain neutral after the invasion; now he had to face the prospect of war with Germany's old adversaries.

Prime Minister's Speech to the Nation

At noon on 3 September Neville Chamberlain informed the nation that Britain's ultimatum to Germany had expired. Germany had not ceased their attack on Poland and as a result, he said 'This country is now at war with Germany. We are ready.' That evening King George VI broadcast to the Commonwealth, stating 'We can only do the right as we see the right, and reverently commit our cause to God'.

Neville Chamberlain.

Germans Cross the Vistula River

The Poles were unable to stop the Germans from crossing the Vistula River on 5 September. The following day the Germans captured Krakow and reached the Romanian border. Polish troops were in retreat and Warsaw was surrounded by 15 September. The following day the Germans demanded surrender, but the Poles refused.

Blitzkrieg

Blitzkrieg, or 'lightning war', was developed by the British in the 1920s and supported by the French and German generals Charles de Gaulle and Heinz Guderian in the 1930s. Originally, tanks were thought only to be of use in seizing ground by brute force, but if allowed to smash through enemy lines front and rear, they could prevent the bloody stalemates of World War I. When they invaded Poland, the German air force, the Luftwaffe, broke up the Polish defences; the Panzer tanks destroyed the enemy's supplies, artillery and supporting units. Blitzkrieg was used in France, the Balkans, Russia and North Africa and was the major contributor to German successes until 1942.

see Soviet Union Invades Poland p. 25

17 September: Sinking of the HMS Courageous

HMS *Courageous* had been built in 1915 and later converted to an aircraft carrier. On 17 September, the German submarine U29 torpedoed her some 240 km (150 miles) off Mizen Head, Ireland. The ship went down in 20 minutes, claiming 518 of her 1,200-man crew, including her captain. The sinking of the ship was the first loss to the Royal Navy, just two weeks into the war.

The HMS *Courageous* was the first naval casualty of the war.

Kriegsmarine (1939–45)

In 1939, the German navy was in no position to challenge the Allied fleets; its major reconstruction plans had just been instituted. When Germany attacked Poland and the war began, all available resources were transferred to the building of U-boats. Despite its comparatively small size, the Kriegsmarine managed to achieve some remarkable results, notably in the destruction of several British warships. Kriegsmarine U-boat successes continued until 1943, by which time Allied technology and tactics were more than a match for them. By the end of the war only two Kriegsmarine major surface vessels were still operational, the rest had been sunk, irreparably damaged or captured.

› see Wolf Packs p. 26

17 September: Soviet Union Invades Poland

Under the terms of the German-Russian Pact of 23 August, Russian troops crossed the Polish border, which was largely undefended. German troops evacuated Lvov and Brest-Litovsk in accordance with the agreement with the Soviets. The Polish government fled to Romania, but the Romanians interned them on 18 September. All Polish territory to the east of the River Bug would be ceded to the Soviets, as per their agreement.

Warsaw Surrenders

Facing little opposition, Russian troops met the German army at Brest-Litovsk; Hitler entered Danzig on 19 September. After days of aerial bombardment, Warsaw surrendered on 27 September and 160,000 Polish troops were captured. The last of the Polish army, having been encircled since 10 September around Modlin and Kutno, finally surrendered on 28 September. Germany now controlled 22 million Poles and the Russians 13 million.

Maginot Line (1929-40)

The Maginot Line, named after the French Minister of War, was intended to protect France for long enough to enable the country to mobilize its armies in the event of war. It stretched from Switzerland to the Ardennes and from the Alps to the Mediterranean, and the Line was

extended along the Belgian border. Within vast defence works and hundreds of kilometres of trenches, thousands of men were strung out along the French border. When the Germans struck, they flooded through the 'impenetrable' Ardennes. When the French surrendered, only one Maginot fort had fallen, yet the garrisons were ordered out without having fired a shot. The Maginot Line had been a failure.

French troops on the Maginot Line.

September: Phoney War

After Britain and France declared war, many expected that the Germans would make a heavy aerial bombing. Britain constructed shelters, distributed gas masks, put ration plans in action and formed voluntary services (Auxiliary Fire Service and Air Raid Precautions). The Women's Voluntary Service (WVS) started stockpiling clothes and blankets for expected refugees. By mid-September 1.5 million people had evacuated major cities. Despite the preparations, no attack occurred and this period became known as the 'Phoney War'.

Wolf Packs (1939–43)

The U-boat had almost won World War I for the Germans, yet the country had just 57 of these submarines, with only 22 operationally effective, when war broke out. Admiral Karl Doenitz envisaged 'wolf packs' of 15–20 U-boats, surrounding and sinking Allied merchant convoys. The number of U-boats increased in the early years of the war and by 1942 there were more than 100. Initial successes saw the sinking of millions of tons of Allied shipping. Doenitz himself estimated that 700,000 tons of Allied shipping needed to be sunk per month in order to starve Britain into submission but the wolf packs struggled to achieve this and as 1943 dawned, Allied anti-submarine warfare and new convoy systems ended the wolf pack's menace.

➧ see Sinking of the HMS Royal Oak p. 27

OCTOBER

This month saw the beginning of Hitler's euthanasia programme, which was a death warrant for anyone the authorities deemed as racially impure. U-boat terror struck again as the unsinkable HMS *Royal Oak* was sunk.

October: Germany Begins Euthanasia Project

Since the Nazis had gained power in Germany in 1933, measures had been taken to ensure 'racial purity', including forced sterilization of those with mental or physical handicaps and the murder of infants. In October 1939 Hitler signed an order authorizing involuntary adult euthanasia. It was signed on his personal stationery to provide doctors with written protection. The programme, overseen by Philipp Bouhler and Karl Brandt, directed them to authorize the euthanasia of primarily non-Jewish Germans. It read: 'Bouhler and Brandt are instructed to broaden the powers of physicians designated by name, who will decide whether those who have – as far as can be humanly determined – incurable illnesses can, after the most careful evaluation, be granted a mercy death.'

14 October: Sinking of HMS Royal Oak

At 27,000 tons, and a cost of £2.5 million, HMS *Royal Oak* was considered virtually unsinkable. Yet on 14 October, the German submarine U47 slipped through the defences at Scapa Flow (Orkney) and sent the *Royal Oak* to the bottom with a salvo of three torpedoes – she was to be the first of the five Royal Navy battleships and battle cruisers sunk during the war. The great battleship went down in 10 minutes, taking 833 of her crew of 1,234. It was an immense morale blow to the Royal Navy and to Britain, demonstrating that the Germans were capable of striking in home waters. Many of the victims were boys aged between 15 and 17; the Royal Navy had a long tradition of sending boys to sea. This practice was largely discontinued after public outcry following the *Royal Oak* disaster.

➧ see Battle of the River Plate p. 29

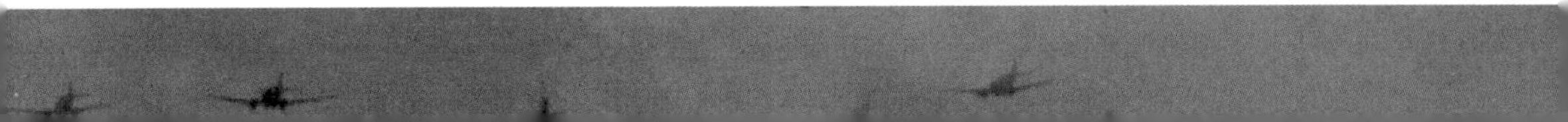

NOVEMBER AND DECEMBER

The failure of the Munich Plot to assassinate Hitler saw all remaining dissenters silenced. The Winter War between Russia and Finland began in freezing conditions. German pocket battleship *Admiral Graf Spree* was sunk during the Battle of the River Plate, and Britain saw the start of a long period of rationing.

8 November: Munich Plot

In a plot hatched by Johann Georg Elser, an anti-Nazi craftsman, a bomb exploded in the Bürgerbräukeller, the Munich beer cellar closely associated with the Nazi party. Having left early, Hitler was spared, but eight people died and 63 were injured. Despite Elser's arrest and confession, Goebbels refused to believe it the work of one man, suspecting a British-led conspiracy and other German dissidents. This accusation allowed Hitler to eradicate any remaining opposition in Germany. The remnants of the left and church and military opposition were eliminated or brought into line.

A Russian soldier during the Winter War.

30 November: Winter War

Despite the continued Russian territorial claims on Finland, the Russian divisions that began crossing the border on 30 September came as a great surprise. The Finns, commanded by Carl Gustaf von Mannerheim, were outnumbered, but they were far superior soldiers to the Russians. By the end of November 27,500 Russians had been killed. Furious at their lack of progress, Joseph Stalin drafted 45 additional divisions. In -30° temperatures the Finns continued to resist, but by February 1940, with 25,000 killed and

43,000 wounded, they were exhausted. The Russo-Finnish Treaty (12 March) saw Finland concede 41,400 sq km (16,000 sq miles) to Russia.

see Soviet Union Invades the Baltic States and Romania p. 41

Admiral Graf Spree (1936–39)

This German vessel was conceived in 1928, but had a small 10,000 ton limit imposed by the Treaty of Versailles. The ship was officially commissioned in 1936 and dubbed a 'pocket battleship' due to her small weight and fighting punch. The ship had advanced prototype diesel engines, an electrically welded hull and massive 11-inch guns. However, the weaknesses of such vessels were their thin armour and decks, a price the German seamen would pay with their lives.

see Allied Forces Enter Norway p. 33

The German battleship *Admiral Graf Spree*, sunk during the Battle of the River Plate.

13–17 December: Battle of the River Plate

The *Admiral Graf Spree* slipped into the South Atlantic to claim more Allied shipping, but was spotted by HMSs *Ajax*, *Exeter* and *Achilles*. The German ship crippled the *Exeter*, but the other two vessels harried her. Langsdorff, the *Graf Spree*'s captain, turned and headed for the neutral port of Montevideo. With the arrival of HMS *Cumberland*, Langsdorff scuttled his own ship in the estuary, bringing to an end the brief Battle of the River Plate.

28 December: Rationing Begins in Britain

By December German U-boat and surface vessel attacks on Allied shipping had accounted for 746,000 tons, with Britain increasingly isolated from its traditional trading partners. Meat rationing was introduced on 28 December, followed by the rationing of bacon, butter and sugar on 8 January 1940. Each household had to register with their local shops and all animal slaughter ceased whilst the government prepared a livestock-control scheme.

see Blitz Begins p. 51

1940

JANUARY–APRIL

As the world entered a new decade, Germany ramped up its manufacture of military equipment. It invaded Norway and Denmark, prompting a fierce Allied response and the Norwegian king and government to flee. Gas masks became a legal requirement in Britain.

January: Germany Steps Up War Production

In direct contravention of the Treaty of Versailles, Germany had already been systematically increasing its production of military equipment. Not only did the country feel it needed to increase the overall strength of its armed forces, but it also needed to establish the necessary mechanisms to accelerate that production in the future. Between 1938 and 1940, for example, bomber production steadily increased by around 100 bombers per year.

8 March: Britain Issues Civilian Gas Masks

Although World War II saw no tactical or strategic use of gas, the British government considered German use of the weapon a distinct possibility. Consequently, from 8 March all civilians and military personnel were systematically issued with gas masks, including equipment for babies and the infirm. It became a legal obligation to carry a gas mask at all times and gas drills became integral parts of air-raid precaution training.

9 April: Germany Invades Denmark and Norway

On 2 April Hitler approved Operation Weserübung, the invasion of Norway and Denmark. By 9 April, nine German divisions, covered by the whole German navy and nearly 500 Luftwaffe aircraft, invaded Denmark; it took them only 48 hours to establish control of the country. They also landed at various points in Norway. Britain and France asked the Belgian government to allow their troops to enter Belgium to try and force the Germans back, but the Belgians refused.

Allied Forces Enter Norway

On 10 April a British flotilla attacked 10 German destroyers at the Norwegian port of Narvik. On 13 April, seven German destroyers were sunk in what became known as the Second Battle of Narvik. The first Allied land units began arriving en masse at Narvik two days later. Additional French units landed later in the month, but by the end of April the Germans, advancing from Oslo and Trondheim, retained virtual control of southern Norway.

➧ see Norway Surrenders p. 39

King Haakon Flees Norway

With the Germans in possession of the majority of the southern half of Norway and all the major population centres, King Haakon and his government were evacuated from Andalsnes aboard HMS *Glasgow* on 29 April. They were initially transported to Tromsos in the Arctic Circle, where they established a provisional capital the following day. By 5 May Haakon and his government were in London as the Norwegian situation continued to deteriorate.

French troops embarking for Norway.

MAY

Dramatic moves in London resulted in Chamberlain's resignation and Winston Churchill taking office. An increasingly confident Germany invaded Belgium and Holland, who quickly surrendered; later in the month they took Boulogne, France, prompting the Dunkirk evacuations of Allied troops.

10 May: Chamberlain Resigns

In the British House of Commons a debate on the Prime Minister's handling of the Norwegian situation led to a vote which was just narrowly won by Chamberlain. There was, however, sufficient opposition to make his position untenable. Labour and Liberal MPs refused to support the government unless Chamberlain resigned. After three days of political manoeuvring, Chamberlain emerged discredited and unable to gather support; he resigned on 10 May.

Churchill Becomes Prime Minister

After Chamberlain's resignation, Winston Churchill became the only viable candidate, having refused to serve under Chamberlain's preferred successor, Lord Halifax, the Foreign Secretary. Churchill retained Chamberlain in the War Cabinet, the Labour leader Clement Attlee became his Deputy Prime Minister and Halifax remained as Foreign Secretary. Churchill brought in the trade union leader, Ernest Bevin, as Minister of Labour, and the powerful Lord Beaverbrook as Minister for Aircraft Production. Churchill told Parliament 'I have nothing to offer but blood, toil, tears and sweat'.

» see Winston Churchill p. 228

Winston Churchill took over the reins as Prime Minister after Chamberlain's resignation in May 1940.

10 May: Germany Invades Belgium and Holland

On 10 May German airborne units began landing around Rotterdam in Holland and on the pivotal Belgian defence point on the River Meuse, near Liège, Fort Eben Emael. In accordance with the Dyle Plan, the French 7th Army and the British Expeditionary Force entered Belgium to take up positions along the River Dyle. The Germans launched heavy bombing raids against Holland and several of the Belgian towns. With German troops crossing the Meuse either side of Sedan, and the Dutch army close to collapse, what had appeared to be an impregnable Allied line looked increasingly vulnerable.

German troops in action after crossing the Meuse in May 1940.

1930s–1945: The Panzers

In firepower, the early German tanks were no match for either the French or British armoured fighting vehicles. They were, however, faster, more manoeuvrable and deployed in concentrated numbers, rather than spread out amongst infantry units as was the British and French case. The German Panzer I was a fast-moving machine-gun unit, whereas the Panzer II and Panzer III had limited firepower of no more than 20 mm (0.8 in). The Germans had acquired the vast Skoda factory and its technically superior 38T tank when they occupied Czechoslovakia, and large numbers of these Czech vehicles were deployed by the German army in their drive through the Lowlands and France.

Eben Emael

The Belgian fortress of Eben Emael was strategically placed on the River Meuse at its junction with the Albert Canal. The fort had been designed to meet every attack – except air. On 11 May, 80 parachutists landed on the roof and blew up the gun casements. The German parachute unit then held the garrison until German ground forces arrived. German gliders secured the two key bridges near the fort and by the next day two Panzer divisions crossed the bridges, precipitating a general Belgian retreat. By 13 May the Germans were poised to swing around the Maginot Line.

» see Belgium Surrenders p. 38

Dutch Monarch Flees to Britain

With the situation in Holland deteriorating quickly, Dutch troops began moving back to 'Fortress Holland', an area that encompassed Amsterdam, The Hague and Rotterdam. On the same day, 13 May, Queen Wilhelmina and her government fled Holland for London. On the following day Dutch forces were ordered to stop fighting as the Germans occupied The Hague in an attempt to seize the royal family.

Germans Bomb Rotterdam

With an overwhelming air superiority, the Germans subjected Rotterdam to a savage bombardment which claimed at least 800 lives. The attacks, which began at around 13:30 on 14 May, succeeded in breaking the resolve of the Dutch. While Allied aircraft attacked German ground forces, anti-aircraft guns claimed some 85 British and French aircraft in the Sedan area. German general Guderian's tanks, by this stage, were almost all across the River Meuse.

A German air force farewell salute before taking off to attack the enemy.

Holland Surrenders

Following the intense bombing of Rotterdam the previous day, at 11:00 on 15 May the Dutch army surrendered to Germany. The front in Belgium appeared to be stabilizing, but by the next day Erwin Rommel's 7th Armoured Division had penetrated 85 km (50 miles) into French territory and was heading for Cambrai, having captured 10,000 prisoners and 100 tanks. Between 17 and 19 May, de Gaulle's 4th Armoured Division attempted to stop Guderian just north of Laon. The counterattack failed and Brussels was declared an open city. Shortly afterwards the Germans took Antwerp.

19 May: Oswald Mosley is Interned

Sir Oswald Mosley, leader of the British Union of Fascists, was arrested and imprisoned along with 33 other prominent Fascists. There was then a series of other arrests and restrictions placed on the movement of 3,000 German-born citizens and 11,000 other aliens. All male aliens were required to report to the police each day and stay at home between 20:00 and 06:00 hours.

➧ see Pétain and Vichy France p. 42

20 May: Germans Reach the English Channel

At around 09:00 on 20 May Guderian took Amiens and 11 hours later his advanced units reached the English Channel at Noyelles, France. Trapped to the north was the French 1st Army, nine divisions of the British Expeditionary Force and the entire Belgian army. The following day, British armour attempted to break through the German lines at Arras. Two French divisions attacked towards Cambrai, but both offensives failed. German forces turned north towards Boulogne and Calais; more Allied counterattacks failed and the Germans continued to advance between 23 and 25 May. There was little coordination between the British, French and Belgian efforts and on 25 May Boulogne fell, trapping the Allied armies.

Dunkirk Evacuates

Codenamed Operation Dynamo, under RAF air cover, the Allies began the evacuation of Dunkirk on 27 May. They extricated 338,266 men, of which 120,000 were French or Belgian.

Famously, a flotilla of around 700 'little ships' – fishing boats, pleasure craft, merchant marine vessels and lifeboats – contributed to the effort, rescuing thousands of men from the beaches. German attacks took place around the perimeter during the evacuation, and some 200 ships were lost during the operation; the British alone left 60,000 trucks and 2,000 guns, as well as thousands of tons of fuel and ammunition. By dawn on 4 June German troops were standing on Dunkirk beach. Bereft of arms and equipment, Churchill realized that the Germans would ultimately attempt to land and take Britain itself. In his immortal speech he said 'We shall fight on the beaches ... we shall fight in the fields ... we shall never surrender'.

Belgium Surrenders

The British and the French were informed that the Belgian army was close to collapse. The Belgian government asked King Leopold to leave the country, but he refused. At 17:00 Leopold sent an envoy to the German headquarters, offering surrender. He received a reply at 22:00, telling him that Hitler demanded an unconditional surrender and Leopold signed at 12:30 on 28 May; this is now repudiated by the Belgian government in Paris.

Matilda (1940–42)

The British infantry tank Matilda.

The first versions of this bizarre-looking tank were slow and new developments only added weight. A new version, the Matilda Senior, was armed with 40-mm Vickers machine guns. Twenty-three Matildas were available to the 7th Armoured Division when they were redeployed in France in May 1940. They proved effective and only heavy German field howitzers anti-aircraft guns could penetrate their armour. After Dunkirk, Matilda IIs became the standard British infantry tank, used extensively in North Africa, Gazala (March 1942) and Tobruk. The Matilda tank was gradually replaced by the Valentine.

JUNE

This was not a good month for the Allies. France suffered German attack on all sides; the French army collapsed, Paris was taken by the Germans and the French government forced to sign an armistice. Norway surrendered to the Germans, and Italy declared war on Britain and France.

5–25 June: Battle of France

On 5 June, preceded by a ferocious bombardment along the River Somme and the Aisne, a series of German thrusts were made on the French lines. By the following day German troops had broken through in the Amiens area and had reached the flank of the Maginot Line. On 7 June the Germans were just short of Rouen on the River Seine and two days later they had occupied the city, as well as Dieppe; they had also reached the River Marne. French troops were in retreat around the Somme and the whole army appeared on the verge of collapse. By 10 June the French government fled as German troops advanced on Paris. The following day Paris was declared an open city and on 14 June German troops entered the capital. Verdun was taken on 15 June and on 17 June Guderian's tanks had almost reached the Swiss border.

9 June: Norway Surrenders

When King Haakon and his government left Tromso aboard the HMS *Devonshire*, heading for the safety of London, the way was clear for a German victory in Norway. On 9 June the last Allied troops left Norway and an armistice came into force there. For the next four years the country would live under German occupation, although it would be ostensibly ruled via Quisling, a Norwegian collaborator with the Germans.

see Germans Occupy Paris p. 40

Norwegian fascist Vidkun Quisling, who supported the German invasion.

10 June: Italy Declares War on Britain and France

With the situation in France deteriorating and the French government leaving Paris for Tours, information was received that Italy would soon throw itself into the arena of war on the German side. At 16:30 on 10 June, the Italian Foreign Minister Ciano informed the French Ambassador that Italy considered itself at war with France, a situation that would come into effect the following day. At 16:45 the Italian minister sent a similar message to the British Ambassador.

» see Italy Invades France p. 41

Italian Bombing Offensive

On 11 June the Italian air force bombed Port Sudan and Aden, while the RAF carried out retaliatory attacks on Italian troops based in Eritrea. Meanwhile the Italians launched eight air raids on Malta. The following day the RAF hit Turin and Genoa. Disaster struck later in the month, though, when Italian anti-aircraft guns shot down the Italian governor of Libya over Tobruk, whilst he was returning from a reconnaissance flight.

13 June: Reynaud Appeals for US Intervention

The French Premier, Paul Reynaud, having turned down calls for an armistice on 12 June, met Winston Churchill for the last time the following day. He sent an urgent appeal to the United States, asking them to 'throw the weight of American power into the scales in order to save France, the advanced guard of democracy'. Reynaud was under increasing pressure from his own council of ministers.

Germans Occupy Paris

With Paris declared an open city at 07:00 on 14 June, German motorcyclists rode into the capital, closely followed by support units. The Armée de Paris had scattered and the French government had fled the capital four days previously. In all, some two million Parisians evacuated the city, harassed on their way by German aircraft. Within a few hours the Swastika was flying from the Eiffel Tower and the Arc de Triomphe and German troops were marching down the Champs Elysée for the first time since 1871. Across the city, cinemas, restaurants and other buildings had signs attached to them, reserving them for German

German troops ride through the conquered French capital.

troops. Any Frenchman who refused to co-operate met immediate, uncompromising force from the Germans.

Italy Invades France

With the Maginot Line breached and the French in retreat, the Italians crossed the Alps and attacked the French on 14 June. By 20 June German units had moved to assist the Italians and on the same day France requested an armistice with Italy. On 22 June the Italians occupied Menton.

see France Signs an Armistice with Italy and Germany p. 42

17 June: Soviet Union Invades the Baltic States and Romania

The Russian army marched into Lithuania unopposed on 17 June in accordance with the agreements they had made with the Germans. Some 35,000 Germans living in Lithuania began moving west. On 21 July Lithuania, Latvia and Estonia agreed to become part of Russia. On 28 June Russian troops crossed the Romanian border to claim Bukovina and Bessarabia. The Romanian King Carol abdicated on 6 September.

22 June: France Signs an Armistice with Italy and Germany

As a final act of humiliation for the French, the Germans insisted that they sign the armistice in the same railway coach in which the Germans received the armistice demands from General Foch in November 1918. Hitler sat on the same chair used by Foch when he presented General Charles Huntziger the document. If anything, it was more punitive than the one Germany had signed in 1918.

The historic railway carriage where the French signed the armistice in June 1940, surrounded by a German guard of honour.

1940–44: Pétain and Vichy France

Vichy France (État Français) was the term used to describe the French government led by Henri Philippe Pétain and based in Vichy (south-east of Paris), which co-operated with Germany between 1940 and 1944. Pétain came to power on 16 June and signed the surrender document on 22 June. France would have an occupied and unoccupied zone; all Jews were to be handed over to the Germans; French prisoners of war would not be released; and the French would bear the cost of the German occupation. The Vichy regime was formally established on 10 July. Pétain remained in power until 20 August 1944. Joseph Darnand, head of the Vichy Milice (police) held an SS rank and pledged allegiance to Germany. He suppressed the Resistance Movement and supported German race laws. The Vichy regime deported over 70,000 Jews and sent 650,000 workers to Germany.

28 June: De Gaulle Becomes Free French Leader

With French troops still fighting the Germans in France, Charles de Gaulle made a radio broadcast in London in which he declared that the war was not over and that the battle for France was a part of the war. He invited all French in England to join him in continuing the struggle but received little support or enthusiasm. The following day he made another broadcast from London, making it clear that he did not support the government of Pétain and would not abide by his decisions. On 23 June he made a further broadcast proposing the creation of the French National Committee. Five days later he was recognized as 'the leader of all free Frenchmen'.

see Charles de Gaulle p. 229

Free French leader Charles de Gaulle.

30 June: Germany Invades the Channel Islands

On 28 June the Channel Islands were partially evacuated and demilitarized and two days later German troops began landing on Jersey and Guernsey. Britain had taken the decision not to contest the two islands, as large numbers of the islanders, their property and animals had already been evacuated. A considerable number of the population chose to stay, as did many police officers and parts of the civilian administration.

see Battle of Britain p. 45

A captured British flag from Guernsey is sent back to Germany.

JULY

The first phase of the Battle of Britain commenced over the English Channel, with German planes attacking British convoys. Hitler broadcast a direct appeal to Britain to surrender, claiming they could not expect to be victors in the conflict.

3 July: British Sink the French Fleet in Oran

The British launched Operation Catapult on 3 July, aiming to prevent the French fleet from falling into German hands. The French commander was given an ultimatum to surrender his ships either to Britain or the US; he failed to respond. Consequently several French ships were sunk or damaged, 1,300 French sailors killed and over 200 French vessels seized in British ports. Following the attack, Pétain's Vichy government broke off diplomatic relations with Britain.

see Allies Attack Dakar p. 53

10 July: Der Kanalkampf

On 10 July, German attacks on the Channel convoys began to intensify; this would signal the first phase of the Battle of Britain. For 10 days the Luftwaffe dropped mines into the harbours and shipping channels at night and attacked the convoys during the day. By 8 August, 18 merchant ships and four Royal Navy destroyers had been lost. By this time, the Luftwaffe had lost some 248 aircraft against 148 RAF losses.

19 July: Hitler Broadcasts a Peace Offer to Britain

Hitler, addressing the Reichstag in Berlin, made a direct and final appeal to Britain: 'If the struggle continues it can only end in annihilation for one of us. Mr Churchill thinks it will be Germany. I know it will be Britain. I am not the vanquished begging for mercy. I speak as a victor. I can see no reason why this war must go on.' see Adolf Hitler p. 234

German leader Adolf Hitler making a radio broadcast.

AUGUST

The Battle of Britain commenced in earnest this month: the Germans' ultimate goal being the invasion of Britain. Luftwaffe and RAF aircraft fought cat-and-mouse battles above the English Channel, resulting in RAF victory and the planned invasion in tatters. The war reached East Africa in August, with Allied troops engaging Italians in Somalia and Sudan.

August: Battle of Britain

The Battle of Britain began in August as the first stage in the German preparations for invading Britain. The Luftwaffe attacks had three objectives: Kanalkampf, to interdict merchant convoys; Adlerangriff, to destroy RAF and warning infrastructure; and Adlertag, to destroy ports and airfields. Between August and September the RAF estimated German losses at 1,600 aircraft with a possible 500 more. Fighter Command had lost around 900 aircraft. Total civilian losses between July and December have been estimated at 23,002 dead and 32,138 wounded. On 19 September, Operation Seelöwe – the planned German invasion – was postponed indefinitely. The victory prompted Churchill to utter the immortal words 'Never in the field of human conflict has so much been owed by so many to so few'. Nonetheless, the Germans came close to overcoming the RAF and only the sudden switch to terror raids on cities gave the RAF their vital breathing space.

August: Operation Seelöwe

The planned German invasion was codenamed Operation Seelöwe ('Sea-Lion') and was designed to be launched in mid-September. Airborne landings in the Dover area would be followed by nine other divisions, which would cross the English Channel in converted river barges. Success required the Luftwaffe to defeat the RAF and then deal with the Royal Navy – any other outcome would mean that the invasion was doomed. Whether Hitler ever took the invasion seriously is unclear; Churchill certainly did not – he actually sent troops to North

Africa during this period. The Luftwaffe failed in their objectives and on 19 September, Operation Seelöwe was indefinitely postponed.

4 August–27 November 1941: War in East Africa

The war officially reached East Africa on 4 August. The Italian attack on British Somalia led to the capture of Berbera on 19 August. The British forces in Sudan launched their counteroffensive on 19 January 1940. Sir William Platt had just two divisions with which to face 17,000 Italians. Aided by Free French troops and fresh British troops, the battle for Keren ended on 27 March, having lasted almost eight weeks. 3,000 Italians were dead and resistance was crushed. The following day the Italians retreated towards Addis Ababa, which fell to the British on 6 April. By now the British had advanced 1,700 miles. The final Italian garrison would surrender on 27 November.

see Renewed German Offensive and Gazala Line p. 107

1935–45: Me109

The Messerschmitt Me109, also known as the BF-109, was the primary German fighter aircraft between 1935 and 1942. For its time it was revolutionary in the sense that it was easy to construct, small and driven by a powerful engine. It is estimated that around 35,000 Me109s had been built by 1945. The Me109s finest hour occurred during the sprawling air battles over the English Channel and southern England in 1940, when the German aces locked horns with the RAF Spitfires and Hurricanes. When handled by an experienced pilot, the Me109 was a highly manoeuvrable aircraft, but it had restricted vision, poor landing and could not be fitted with heavy armaments without affecting its speed and handling.

see Me110 p. 48

The German Messerschmitt Me109

8 August: Adlerangriff

Stuka planes in the German Luftwaffe on a raid.

Codenamed Adlerangriff ('Attack of the Eagles'), Hitler ordered Goering's Luftwaffe to destroy the RAF. Luftwaffe squadrons were concentrated around the Calais region in preparation, but the British had already cracked the enigma codes and were decoding the German squadrons' orders. Early on 8 August, 300 Stukas and 150 Me109s headed for a British convoy en route to Swanage in Dorset. The plan was to draw out the RAF and destroy them over the Channel. Several Spitfire and Hurricane squadrons engaged the Me109s while the Stukas hit the ships. Another Luftwaffe attack took place at around 16:30 with over 150 German aircraft involved. RAF losses had been 13, Luftwaffe losses 16.

German Stuka planes.

1937–45: Stuka

The Junkers Ju87 'Stuka', known to the Germans as Sturzkampfbomber, was a dive bomber, effective against ships and tanks; full-scale production began in 1937. The Stuka had proved to be devastating in Poland, France and the Low Countries, but over the English Channel and southern England it was no match for the Spitfire or the Hurricane. Its primary role was to break up enemy concentrations, paving the way for German ground troops. The Stuka had a maximum speed of just 314 kph (195 mph) and a range of 320 km (199 miles), making it easy prey for most Allied fighters. Whole squadrons of the Stuka were destroyed by the RAF and they were withdrawn from the area of operations, but continued in action elsewhere.

11 August: Germans Target Radar Stations

On 11 August the first major German air offensive was ready to begin. The Luftwaffe could muster 2,669 bombers and 933 fighters (Me109s). Against this was ranged 704 RAF fighters, over 600 of which were Hurricanes and Spitfires. The RAF also had 350 bombers. On the same day the Germans began daytime attacks on radar stations in the south-east and along the south coast of Britain.

1936–45: Me110

The Me110, or Messerschmitt BF110, was originally designed as a fighter plane to clear the path of incoming bomber streams. The aircraft was nicknamed the 'Destroyer'. It was used to some effect against Channel convoys, but it was no match for Spitfires or Hurricanes. It was reduced to the role of fighter bomber due to its long range (1,720 km/1,070 miles) with a speed of 467 kph (290 mph). The BF110C saw the most service during the Battle of Britain, where it suffered heavily at the hands of RAF pilots. This version of the aircraft had a maximum speed of 402 kph (250 mph).

An Me110.

13 August: Adlertag

Codenamed Adlertag ('Eagle Day'), this was the phase of the Battle of Britain that saw an intensification of raids against key air-defence targets. The raids, launched on 13 August, were the heaviest the Luftwaffe had been able to muster. In excess of 1,400 German aircraft flew over the English Channel in waves, ordered to destroy all RAF airbases in south-east England, paving the way for Operation Sealion. Despite being hugely outnumbered, the RAF accounted for 45 German aircraft losses with just 13 of its own. All but two of the RAF bases were saved. The pounding continued until, just as the RAF was on its knees, the Luftwaffe began air attacks on London. The RAF recovered and it became evident that the invasion would never happen; after four months of raids, the Luftwaffe had failed.

1938–45: Spitfire

The Spitfire was based on the Supermarine S6B seaplane and came into service with the RAF in 1938. It was continually modified, the first version having a speed of 580 kph (360 mph) and the last, the Spitfire XIV, 710 kph (440 mph). The initial orders, placed before September 1939, amounted to 1,160. By the end of the war, some 20,000 had been built The Spitfire became immortalized as the symbol of British resistance and resolve in the darkest times of the war.

The British Spitfire.

21 August: 'Never in the Field of Human Conflict'

On 21 August, as the RAF held off the German Luftwaffe in the skies over the English Channel, Winston Churchill delivered a defiant speech, recognizing that this war depended on organization, strategy, science and morale. He gave his utmost praise to the RAF, saying 'Never in the field of human conflict was so much owed by so many to so few. All hearts go out to the fighter pilots, whose brilliant actions we see with our own eyes day after day, but we must never forget that all the time ... our bomber squadrons travel far into Germany, find their targets in the darkness by the highest navigational skill, aim their attacks, with deliberate, careful precision, and inflict shattering blows upon the ... structure of the Nazi power.'

Britain's First Bombing Raid on Berlin

In retaliation for attacks on London, the RAF dropped bombs and leaflets over Berlin on the night of 25 August, remaining over the city for three hours. Although the raid was ineffective, it shocked the Germans and Hitler was furious with Goering, who had promised that such a raid could never take place. It was a great boost to British morale.

➧ see Hitler Begins the Blockade of Britain p. 52

An RAF attack during the Battle of Britain.

SEPTEMBER

After a year of war, the long-expected attacks on Britain began with the German 'blitz' of London and other major UK cities. The US passed an act that would allow them to raise an army if required. Italy invaded Egypt, and Hitler switched tactics to concentrate on blocking vital supplies reaching Britain in a bid to starve the nation into surrender. The Tripartite Pact was signed between Italy, Germany and Japan.

7 September: Blitz Begins

From July the Luftwaffe concentrated its efforts on eliminating the RAF by targeting radar stations, aircraft factories, airfields and tackling RAF fighters in the air. This period, known as the Battle of Britain, had been a failure, but the RAF was on the verge of collapse. Suddenly, on 7 September, the Luftwaffe changed its tactics and began to target London, signalling the beginning of the Blitz. On the first day, 430 civilians were killed and 1,600 wounded; another 412 were killed the following day. Although the Blitz would continue at a lower intensity throughout the war years, it is the period up to May 1941 that signifies the Blitz phase.

see Bombing of Coventry p. 58

British civilians salvage what they can from the wreckage during the Blitz.

German Targets

During this time 130 large-scale night raids were made on Britain, some 71 against London alone. Other targets included key industrial cities across the country. The Blitz claimed the lives of some 60,000 civilians; a further 87,000 were injured and two million homes were destroyed. London was worst hit with 60 per cent of the casualties and damage. By the time the war had reached its mid-point, the number of British civilian deaths had outweighed losses in military manpower.

12 September: Italy Invades Egypt

On the night of 12 September, Italian troops crossed the Egyptian border from Libya and occupied Sollum. Within four days they had reached Sidi Barrani, despite heavy losses as a result of RAF bombing. On 25 September British aircraft raided Tobruk and their naval forces bombarded Sidi Barrani. Italian forces were static and when Hitler met with Italian leader Mussolini at the beginning of the following month, he offered Italy military aid in North Africa; Mussolini declined.

see Rudolfo Graziani p. 232

16 September: US passes the Selective Service Act

The Selective Service Act, established on 16 September, was the first US peacetime draft in the country's history. Significantly, under US law, this was not 'involuntary servitude' under the terms of the 13th Amendment, but rather the US Congress's right to raise and support an army. Remarkably, and again for the first time in US history, African-American troops would be included in the drafts. 16.1 million US citizens would serve.

see Roosevelt is Re-Elected p. 57

17 September: Hitler Begins the Blockade of Britain

With the Luftwaffe unable to eliminate the RAF, let alone bomb Britain into submission, Hitler realized that the prospect of launching an invasion was slipping through his fingers. By coordinating the U-boat effort, the judicious use of German surface vessels and continued pressure from the Luftwaffe, he intended to starve Britain into submission. At the very least, Hitler hoped that he could render Churchill unable to take any action against German interests in Europe or elsewhere. Indeed, without food and materials support from North America and beyond, the island had little long-term hope of being able to feed or defend itself.

23 September: Allies Attack Dakar

The attack on Vichy-held Dakar was de Gaulle's first major operation. He had hoped that the Vichy would offer no resistance in West Africa. At 07:00 on 23 September he made a radio broadcast, asking for permission to land. He repeated it an hour later and then made a third request. At 10:50 Vichy coastal batteries opened up and attempts to land were checked. The action was called off.

27 September: Tripartite Pact

The Tripartite Pact, signed between Germany, Italy and Japan, on 27 September, was ratified in Berlin. The pact obliged the three countries to come to one another's military assistance in the case of any attack by a country not already involved in the war. The Italians and Germans would have a free hand to establish a new order in Europe, while the Japanese would have similar freedoms in Asia.

see Italy Fails in Greece p. 56

Axis leaders give the fascist salute after signing the Tripartite Pact.

OCTOBER

Franco offered Hitler his country's support, which he declined; Spain remained neutral throughout the conflict. Sixteen million citizens were mobilized in the US as a result of the previous month's Service act. Italy invaded Greece, as part of a measure to force Greece to accept Italian occupation.

7 October: Germans Enter Romania

German troops entered Romania on the pretext of restructuring the Romanian military, but in fact they were hoping to secure the Romanian oil wells. Five days later Mussolini learned of the coup and reportedly said 'Hitler always presents me with a *fait accompli*, but this time I shall pay him back in his own coin. When he reads the papers he'll see that I've occupied Greece, and that will make us all square.'

▸ see Italy Fails in Greece p. 56

16 October: Americans Register for the Draft

The 1940 Selective Service Act had netted the US with around 16 million men by 16 October of that year. Ultimately around 8.5 million would be assigned to the US army, 3.5 to the US navy and half a million to the marines. These men would assume largely front-line duties. The remainder and large numbers of women would be assigned non-combat or specialized duties. The US had mobilized in a way never seen before.

23 October: Hitler Meets Franco

The Spanish leader Francisco Franco offered his country's support to join the Axis Powers in June, but the Germans showed little interest in his help at the time. On 23 October, Hitler finally agreed to meet Franco at Hendaye, near the Franco-Spanish border, and offered him the British-owned Gibraltar, but was not prepared to provide for the Spanish army or to ensure Franco a North African empire. As it transpired, Allied food and fuel kept Spain neutral and Franco only provided the Germans with submarine refuelling bases and other minor assistance.

24 October: Pétain meets Hitler

The meeting between Hitler and French leader Pétain at Montoire on 24 October has been the subject of much controversy. Many claim that Pétain was trying to protect France from severe destruction until such time as Germany was defeated. He offered co-operation in return for peace and the retention of the French empire. Pétain also hoped that France could be transformed into a 'stable authoritarian order based on work, family, Fatherland'.

Pétain returned to France in April 1945 and was arrested for treason. He was tried and sentenced to death, but his venerable age and previous services to the French nation saved him from the hangman. He died in prison in 1951.

see Henri-Phillipe Pétain p. 240

Hitler and Pétain meet to discuss the future of France.

28 October–1 March 1941: Italy Fails in Greece

At 03:00 on 28 October the Italians delivered an ultimatum to the Greek government, demanding that Greece accept Italian occupation for the duration of the war in order to ensure Greek neutrality. The Greek Prime Minister Metaxas took this to be a declaration of war and at dawn the same day Italian troops crossed the Greek border. Greek resistance through early November continued and they began counterattacking. Lack of transport and armour prevented the Greeks from exploiting the Italian weaknesses, but by January the Greeks had reached Albania. On 23 February the Greeks accepted Britain's offer of military assistance. Although seriously outnumbered, the Greeks were still making headway when, on 7 March, the first British troops began arriving at Piraeus. Seven days later the last Italian attempt at Greek submission failed.

see British Arrive in Greece p. 65

Italian soldiers in Greece; the Italians failed in their attempts to suppress the Greeks, who were assisted by the arrival of British troops.

NOVEMBER AND DECEMBER

In November, Roosevelt was voted in for an historic third term as US president. The end of the year also saw much fierce fighting: the Italian fleet at Taranto, in the Mediterranean, was destroyed by the British; Britain's car manufacturing centre, Coventry, was destroyed in a devastating German air-raid; and Hungary, Romania and Slovakia joined the Axis powers. The British launched their offensive against Italian troops in North Africa.

5 November: Roosevelt is Re-Elected

US President Roosevelt romped home to victory over his Republican rival Wendell Wilkie and became the first US President in the country's history to be re-elected for a third term. Roosevelt mustered 27 million votes to Wilkie's 22 million, although Roosevelt's share of the vote at 54.7 per cent was lower than his 1936 high of 60.8 per cent. Accusations describing Roosevelt as a dictator fell on deaf electoral ears.

see Franklin D. Roosevelt p. 242

US President Franklin D. Roosevelt.

11 November: Hitler Meets Molotov

The meeting between Hitler and the Russian Foreign Minister, Vyacheslav Molotov, in November has often been cited as the reason why Germany turned on its erstwhile ally. Molotov was already intriguing in Romania and Hitler suspected that the Russians were behind the anti-German uprising in Yugoslavia. From this point Hitler paid close attention to the Russians, probably realizing conflict was inevitable.

11 November: Taranto

By November, the British Mediterranean Fleet was facing the task of defending a 3,220-km (2,000-mile) supply route from Gibraltar to Alexandria, via Malta. The obstacle was the powerful Italian fleet situated at Taranto. At 20:40 on 11 November, the first of 12 Swordfish aircraft left HMS *Illustrious*, and arrived over Taranto at 22:56. Their first victim was the 29,000-ton battleship *Conte di Cavour*; two torpedoes hit the *Littorio*, while more aircraft tackled the Italian cruisers, destroyers and submarines. A second wave arrived over the harbour, claiming the *Caio Duillio*. For the loss of only two aircraft, the Italian fleet had been mauled; it fled for the safety of Naples harbour. Chillingly, the attack on Taranto became the blueprint for the Japanese attack on Pearl Harbor.

1936–45: Flying String Bags

The Swordfish aircraft known as the Flying String Bag came into service with the Fleet Air Arm in 1936. Despite its World War I appearance, it outclassed all other aircraft that were developed to replace it and consequently stayed in service throughout the war. The aircraft was designed as a torpedo attack or reconnaissance aircraft. Some 2,391 were built and its most glorious moment during the war took place during the naval Battle of Taranto. Only 21 Swordfish were involved in the sortie but they managed to destroy three battleships, a cruiser, two destroyers and other ancillary vessels.

see Sinking of the Bismark p. 79

14 November: Bombing of Coventry

During the night of 14 November, arguably the worst Luftwaffe air raid outside London took place when the British city of Coventry was carpet-bombed. The Germans intended to destroy the city's productive capacity, as even then it was the centre of the British automobile industry. After the attack, the Germans coined their own word, 'coventrisieren' which meant to annihilate, or raze to the ground. Some 449 German aircraft were involved in the raid, dropping around 600 tons of high explosives and thousands of incendiary bombs.

The British city of Coventry was razed to the ground by the Luftwaffe.

By November the weekly death toll from German raids had fallen to 3,000 from a previous high of around 6,000. After the war, Coventry was twinned with the similarly devastated Dresden.

20–23 November: Hungary Enters the War

On 20 November 1940 Count Teleki, the Hungarian Prime Minister, and his Foreign Minister, Count Casaky, signed the necessary documents linking Hungary to the German-Japanese-Italian Tripartite Pact. Effectively Hungary had joined the war. On 23 November Romania followed suit and the following day Slovakia became involved in the conflict. Hungary and Romania would provide Germany with much-needed manpower and industry.

➧ see Germany Invades the Soviet Union p. 81

9 December: British Launch an Offensive in North Africa

After taking Sidi Barrani on 16 September, the Italians took no further action. British commander Archibald Wavell began his offensive and broke through the lines with just two divisions against seven Italian formations. In just four days of fighting, four Italian divisions were obliterated and 38,000 prisoners taken. The haul included 1,000 trucks, over 70 tanks and 237 guns. By 12 December the only Italians remaining on Egyptian soil were prisoners. By 25 December the prisoner tally had reached 35,949. Continued attacks led to the fall of Bardia and another 40,000 prisoners. By 20 January Hitler had decided to send German troops to North Africa. The Italians continued to retreat towards Benghazi and a further 20,000 men were captured at Beda Fomm.

➧ see Archibald Wavell p. 244

1941

JANUARY AND FEBRUARY

The Allies had a successful start to the year when they captured the garrison of Tobruk in Libya. This was a precursor to a catastrophic Italian defeat by the British, the Battle of Beda Fomm, in February. February also saw the first deportation of Jews to concentration camps by the Germans.

5 January: Allies Enter Libya and Capture Tobruk

Allied forces entered Libya on 5 January and British troops began attacking Tobruk on 21 January. After one day the garrison surrendered and the British captured 30,000 prisoners, 70 tanks and 200 guns. By 1 February the Italians had abandoned Benghazi and on 6

British troops and tanks wait to enter a burning Tobruk.

February, after destroying 80 Italian tanks, the Australians led the entry into Benghazi and the British prepared for the battle of Beda Fomm.

Battle of Beda Fomm

The Battle of Beda Fomm on 2 February was a catastrophic Italian defeat that took place 190 km (120 miles) south of Benghazi. Advanced elements of the British 7th Armoured Division managed to cut across the desert and block the retreating Italian 10th Army. During the battle, in which the Italians were ambushed, some 25,000 prisoners were captured. The British offensive was over, with 500 dead, 55 missing and 1,373 wounded. Thirty-thousand British troops had advanced 800 km (500 miles) in two months, destroying 10 divisions and taking 130,000 captives. Graziani was relieved and replaced by Garibaldi, who dug in and awaited the drive on Tripoli – which never came.

12 February: Rommel Takes Command of the Afrika Korps

Rommel arrived in Tripoli two days before the advanced guard of his Afrika Korps. He was given the task of rescuing the Italian forces that had suffered a series of defeats against the British in North Africa. As it transpired, the arrival of German forces stiffened Italian resolve and soon Rommel was forced on the offensive, taking his initiative from the British.

➧ see Germans Launch an Offensive in North Africa p. 67

16 February: Jews are Deported from Vienna

Around 10,000 Jews from Vienna and the surrounding area were earmarked for deportation under the Madagascar Plan. Deportation in the first 18 months of the war was the centrepiece of dealing with Jews as far as the Nazis were concerned. In the Vienna area the pre-war Jewish population had been 166,000, 100,000 of whom emigrated before the war. The remainder were deported to concentration camps. After the invasion of Russia, it became clear that the means of dealing with Russian Jews (mobile firing squads) could not be used on western Jews and it was decided to deport them east to extermination camps.

➧ see SS Begins Mass Murders p. 82

MARCH

The Nazis' Final Solution moved one step further with the opening of the concentration camps in Poland in March. The US Lend-Lease Act was passed this month, benefiting the Allies in their fight against the Axis powers, which grew in strength when Yugoslavia signed the Tripartite Act. The conflict grew more serious in North Africa, with Rommel's Afrika Corps facing a depleted Allied army.

1 March: Extermination Camps Become Operational

The Germans constructed six concentration camps in Poland, the largest of which – Auschwitz-Brikenau – was officially opened on 1 March 1941. By the time it closed in 1944 1.4 million Jews had been murdered there. The system of deporting Jews to the six key extermination camps (Auschwitz-Brikenau, Auschwitz, Chelmno, Belzec, Sobibor and Treblink) became the standard method of dealing with Jews and these camps would account for 3.5 million lives. Belzec also came into operation in March 1941, Sobibor in April and Treblink in July. Their existence was considered an utmost secret and only a handful of the prisoners ever managed to escape. These camps can be differentiated from the other concentration camps in that their sole purpose was for execution; they did not have facilities for slave labour.

➧ see Goering Presents the Final Solution p. 85

3 March: Lend-Lease Act

On 3 March US Congress passed the necessary legislation to allow President Roosevelt to sell, transfer, exchange or lend military equipment to countries engaged in fighting against the Axis powers. Some 38 countries would be the beneficiaries of this aid, worth some $50 billion; Britain would be the main borrower ($31 billion). The move had been prompted by events in July 1940 when Britain had lost 11 destroyers in 10 days. Churchill had requested

The infamous concentration camp at Auschwitz in Poland.

immediate assistance from Roosevelt and the President responded by exchanging 50 destroyers for 99-year leases on British bases in the Caribbean and Newfoundland.

see Atlantic Charter p. 87

7 March: British Arrive in Greece

In response to the agreement with the Greeks, the British Expeditionary Force began arriving at Piraeus and Volos on 7 March. Britain had promised 100,000 troops but in the event could only commit 57,000 or four divisions, two of which were armoured. In the wake of the successful British offensive against the Italians in North Africa, the redeployment could not have come at a worse time; only a month previously Rommel had taken command.

see Germany Invades Yugoslavia and Greece p. 69

25 March: Yugoslavia Enters the War

On 19 March the Germans had issued an ultimatum to Yugoslavia to allow them to pass through Yugoslav territory and join the Tripartite Pact. In return they would be given Thessaloniki and parts of Greek Macedonia. On 20 March Yugoslavia agreed in principle and despite a British warning on 24 March, signed the Tripartite Act the following day in Vienna, with Hitler, Ribbentrop and the Japanese Ambassador present.

see Germany Invades Yugoslavia and Greece p. 69

30 March: Axis Vessels are Seized

On 27 March meetings in Washington between British and American military advisors closed and a strategy was formed in the event of the US entering the war. Three days later the United States, Mexico, Costa Rica and Venezuela took all German, Italian and Danish ships berthed in their harbours into protective custody. By this stage the exchange of information between Britain and the US had reached a wartime footing.

see Greenland is Placed Under US Control p. 70

German tanks in Libya.

30 March: Germans Launch an Offensive in North Africa

Having spent a month in North Africa, Rommel made his first move on 24 March, when he reoccupied El Agheila, on the border between Tripolitania and Cyrenaica. He launched his first counteroffensive six days later, with a combination of German and Italian forces. They engaged British troops at Mersa Brega, forcing the British to withdraw, having lost 80 armoured vehicles. By 2 April Rommel had retaken Agedabia and Zuetina, forcing the British to evacuate Benghazi. Rommel's Afrika Korps was still under strength but he was facing a much-depleted British and Commonwealth force that had seen most of its experienced troops and commanders transferred to operations in Greece. Rommel would continue to advance on the shocked enemy.

1941–43: Rommel's Afrika Korps

Rommel's Afrika Korps came into existence in 1941 as the German contribution to the North African war effort. Throughout the war units including the 10th Panzer, 15th Panzer, 90th Light and 164th Light remained integral parts of the Afrika Korps. They were to accompany Rommel across the width of North Africa with his first offensive in April 1941, contend with the British operations Brevity and Battleaxe and then resume the offensive once more between late 1941 and 1942. Most of the units also fought during Operation Crusader, Alam el Halfa and resisted Montgomery during Lightfoot but were decisively defeated during Supercharge. They were then pursued across North Africa, only to discover that Allied forces had landed in Tunisia; many of them would fall into captivity by 1943. At the time of the surrender and the break-up of the Afrika Korps, Rommel was no longer in command. He had been replaced by General Von Arnim. Many of the units would continue to exist and some found themselves posted to the Eastern Front or back under Rommel's command, not as the Afrika Korps, but as mobile units positioned behind the main defence lines along the French or Belgian coasts, aiming to prevent Allied landings.

see Erwin Rommel p. 241

APRIL

Early April saw the Allied forces in North Africa besieged in Tobruk after facing strong German opposition. With no declaration of war, German forces invaded Greece and Yugoslavia; both countries quickly surrendered. The Soviets and Japan signed a non-aggression pact. Greenland was placed under US control, aiding Allied convoys crossing the North Atlantic.; in the Middle East, British forces secured Baghdad.

4–10 April: Germans Capture Benghazi and Besiege Tobruk

British and Commonwealth troops, under orders to withdraw should they encounter any serious Axis opposition, began to retire eastwards, allowing Rommel to enter Benghazi. He continued to push forward from 4 April, capturing the British General O'Connor and General Neame, and taking Derna three days later. By 10 April Allied troops had withdrawn to Tobruk and were cut off from the rest of the army.

» see Renewed German Offensive and Gazala Line p. 107

The Germans enter Benghazi.

6–16 April: Germany Invades Yugoslavia and Greece

At 05:15 on 6 April German forces invaded Yugoslavia and Greece, attacking the former with no declaration of war. The attacks were supported by Hungarian and Italian units. The cause of the invasion had been the overthrow of the pro-German government in Yugoslavia and Hitler had moved quickly to eliminate the chance of Allied occupation. By 8 April the Yugoslav army was on the verge of collapse and the Germans were advancing on all fronts. Zagreb fell on 10 April, Nis and Skopjy had already fallen, denying the Greeks or the British the opportunity of assisting the Yugoslavs. Belgrade fell on 12 April and by 17 April the Yugoslavian army had been destroyed and the last centre of resistance in Bosnia had collapsed. More than 300,000 prisoners had been taken.

see Yugoslavia and Greece Surrender p. 70

German troops advancing through Serbia, Yugoslavia, after the invasion.

1941–45: Jasenovac

Jasenovac was a concentration-camp complex established some 100 km (62 miles) south of Zagreb. Unlike the other camps, it was set up and administered by the pro-German Croatians. Jasenovac, dubbed 'the Auschwitz of the Balkans' was run by feared Ustaska security police. Various estimates have been made of the number of Serbs, Jews and gypsies murdered at Jasenovac, but it was certainly no less than 85,000. This was just one part of the overall genocide in Yugoslavia as at least 600,000 Serbs were murdered by the regime (around a third of the pre-war Serb population). The camps were liberated by Tito's partisans in April 1945; few came to trial for their crimes.

10 April: Greenland Placed Under US Control

Having reached an agreement with the Danish government, US troops began occupying Greenland as part of the US policy to deny the Germans the North Atlantic and to protect the ever-growing numbers of convoys carrying war supplies to Britain. The Atlantic Fleet Support Group of the US navy began operating out of Greenland in order to deal with the growing threat of the German navy.

see Roosevelt Orders the Freezing of German Assets p. 80

13 April: Soviet-Japanese Non-Aggression Pact Signed (1941)

The Japanese Foreign Minister Matsuoko – having met Hitler in Berlin on 4 April, where they discussed the possibility of an attack on Singapore and an impending conflict with the US – moved on to Moscow on 13 April. Here he signed a five-year non-aggression treaty with the Russian Foreign Minister, Molotov. Japan was putting in place the last pieces of the jigsaw of support and neutrality they needed.

see Soviets Denounce the Pact with Japan p. 208

17–23 April: Yugoslavia and Greece Surrender

Yugoslavia surrendered officially on 17 April and on the following day German troops pushed past Mount Olympus, threatening to cut off British troops. Meanwhile Italian and other German troops broke through Greek lines and by 20 April they were surrounded. Officially Greek resistance ended the following day, when 16 divisions surrendered. Two days later, for the cameras – and on Hitler's orders – the Greek surrender was repeated near Thessaloniki.

see Athens Falls p. 71

German tanks in Athens.

17 April–1 June: Britain Launches Offensive and Captures Baghdad

On 4 April 1941, the pro-German Rashid Ali seized control in Iraq. On 17 April British troops crossed the border and on 2 May they clashed with Iraqi troops at Habbaniyah; within two days they had occupied Bazra. By the end of the month Baghdad was surrounded and Rashid Ali surrendered (replaced by Emi Abdullah). British troops entered Baghdad the following day, securing this strategically important region.

» see British Occupy Syria and Enter Iran with Soviets p. 84

Troops completing a bridge after the capture of Baghdad.

27 April: Athens Falls

Despite the Greek surrender, many units continued to fight alongside the British. German paratroops began landing on Greek islands on 24 April and two days later they captured Corinth on the mainland. British troops continued their retreat, embarking from several Greek ports. Athens fell on April 27 and the last British troops left the following day, bound for Crete, leaving nearly 13,000 men behind.

» see Battle for Crete p. 78

MAY

In early May, Stalin became Premier of the Soviet Union. Early May also saw the RAF and Luftwaffe carry out numerous raids on key targets in each country, including the last major attack on London by the Germans. The battle for the territorially important Crete commenced, with the German army securing victory. On the sea, the Allies lost HMS *Hood* while the German ship *Bismark* sank with great loss of life.

6 May: Stalin Becomes Premier of the Soviet Union

On 6 May the Russian Praesidium of the Supreme Soviet nominated Joseph Stalin to become President of the Council of People's Commissars. Stalin already held the rank of Communist Party Secretary and in this deft manoeuvre he was able to secure even more power. He was now better able to enforce his own policies and visions of Russia, its future and its strength and power.

see Joseph Stalin p. 242

8 May: RAF Launches a Bomber Offensive on Germany

On 7 May the Germans bombed the Humber area of Britain heavily; the following night, in retaliation, British bombers carried out a massive raid on Hamburg. The same night German bombers were back over the Humber region and also made attacks on London. On 9 May the RAF hit Bremen but the following evening a number of key targets in London were hit.

The result of the British bombing raid on Hamburg.

1936–68: Bomber Command

Bomber Command was formed on 14 July 1936 in Buckinghamshire and was formally disbanded on 30 April 1968. It has been estimated that between 3 September 1939 and 8 August 1945 RAF Bomber Command flew some 387,416 sorties, dropped 955,000 tons of bombs and lost 8,953 aircraft and 55,573 personnel. Typically, a crew member would serve a tour of duty of 30 operations. Statistically it was nearly impossible to survive this number of missions, yet many did. Bomber Command initially used aircraft such as the Wellington, the Hampden, the Blenheim and the Whitley. Undoubtedly the most famous of the heavy bombers used was the Lancaster, which was used on the famous Dambuster raid. The Halifax came into operation in 1944 and was considered to be one of the finest of their aircraft. Bomber Command hit enemy-occupied targets across the length and breadth of Europe throughout the war. The last attack took place on 24 April 1945.

see Arthur 'Bomber' Harris p. 232

10 May: Hess Flies to Scotland

Rudolf Hess parachuted from an Me110 into the village of Eaglesham, near Glasgow, to deliver a peace plan to the Duke of Hamilton, whom he had met at the 1936 Berlin Olympic Games. Once it became clear that Hess was not speaking on behalf of Hitler, Churchill dismissed any suggestions of peace. The Germans claimed that he had been suffering from hallucinations and was mentally disordered. Hess was imprisoned in Buchanan Castle, the Tower of London and then in Abergavenny. At the time Hess's arrival was a sensation as it pointed to dissention within the ranks of the Nazi Party.

see Rudolf Hess p. 233

Rudolf Hess.

1939–45: The Secret War

The desire to know what the enemy was doing reached incredible heights during the war. In Britain, MI5 and MI6 were inextricably involved, but there were many other smaller organizations committing espionage, undertaking covert operations and using new communications technology. There was also the fascinating world of codes and ciphers, in which both sides attempted to ensure that their most secret information and orders were not compromised by the enemy. Equally as fascinating were the various Special Forces which fought a semi-covert war, at least in as much as they were primarily designed as information gatherers, kidnappers or raiders. Britain had its own Special Air Service and Long Range Desert Group, and across occupied Europe there were members of the Special Operations Executive guiding foreign nationals against the enemy. Perhaps the best-kept secret of the war was the development of the atomic bombs in the US, known as the Manhattan Project.

Bletchley Park

In the summer of 1939, a group of scholars recruited as code-breakers arrived at Bletchley Park. Their mission was to break the German Enigma cipher, considered to be an unbreakable code. The odds against them were a staggering 150,000,000,000,000,000,000:1. The team built Colossus, the world's first computer, to crack the code used by the German military. The work at Bletchley Park has been said to have shortened the war by at least two years. At the height of the operations at Bletchley Park, 10,000 people were engaged in deciphering German codes. Everything was carried out in secrecy, Churchill himself saying of those there that they were 'the geese that laid the golden eggs and never cackled'.

Bletchley Park, where the Enigma code was finally cracked.

1918–45: Enigma

The German Enigma machine was invented in 1918 and was originally used for secured banking communications. A letter could be typed into a machine which sent electrical impulses through a series of rotating wheels, contacts and wires to produce the ciphered letter. The machine operator who received the message would have to type in the code and then see the deciphered message light up letter by letter on the keyboard. Polish intelligence had broken the code in 1932 and prior to September 1939 the cipher was only changed once every few months. German operator mistakes and the acquisition of an Enigma machine finally allowed the decryption teams, led by Alan Turing, to break the code. Intercept stations collected German radio traffic which was decoded and then sent to the military.

Enigma machine.

10 May: Chetniks Begin Resistance Against the Germans

The Chetniks were Serbian royalists who formed guerrilla groups to resist Axis occupation and the pro-German Croatian government. They were led by Draza Mihailovic, and their desire was to liberate Yugoslavia and restore the monarchy. The Chetnik base was at Ravna Gora and for them and Tito's Partisans in the early months it was very much a question of survival; both struggled to win support.

» see Chetniks Battle with Tito p. 92

10 May: Last Major German Attack on London

After nine months of the Blitz, 550 Luftwaffe aircraft dropped hundreds of high explosive and an estimated 100,000 incendiaries on London. Civilian casualties were estimated at around 1,400, making this the biggest German raid since the beginning of the war. The RAF accounted for 29 German aircraft and it seemed that the damage to civilian homes, the Houses of Parliament, Westminster Abbey, St Paul's Cathedral and the British Museum was the beginning of a new phase. In fact this turned out to be the last major raid on London: the high point of the Luftwaffe's attempt to crush Britain had now passed. In all an estimated 20,000 Londoners were killed and 25,000 injured during the war.

St Paul's Cathedral in London stands among smoking ruins.

» see Blitz Begins p. 51

1935–45: Luftwaffe

The German Luftwaffe was created in May 1935, following the denunciation of the Treaty of Versailles. The 100,000-man Reichswehr became the Wehrmacht and consisted of an army, a navy and an air force. Between 1939 and 1945 3.4 million Germans served in the Luftwaffe. Of these an estimated 165,000 were killed, 155,000 missing and 192,000 wounded. Training had taken place in secret in Russia and its pilots were some of the best to fly in the war. Of the 7,361 men awarded the highest German honour, the Knight's Cross, 1,785 were from the Luftwaffe.

see Luftwaffe Bombs Moscow p. 85

A German Luftwaffe pilot with his Stuka plane.

1940–45: Battle of the Atlantic

From the opening day of the war the German navy sought to cut off Europe from the United States and its other trading partners. Indeed by 1 October 1939 they had already sunk 153,000 tons of merchant shipping. In 1940 Britain needed 120,000 tons of food and fuel each day in order to survive. This pressure intensified after the fall of mainland Europe. When the US first entered the war they had little success against the German navy; U-boats were being delivered at a rate of 30 each month and in June the Allies lost 173 ships. By March 1943 400 U-boats were in action, but by July the Allies were sinking German ships faster than they could build them, while the Germans were sinking less than the Americans could construct. By May 1945, U-boats had sunk 3,500 merchant ships, 2,500 of which were in the North Atlantic. Three-quarters of the German U-boats had also been lost.

➧ see Wolf Packs p. 26

20–31 May: Battle for Crete

The island of Crete had assumed importance by the middle of 1941 due to its position midway between Europe and Egypt; possession was vital for the struggle for North Africa. After air raids on the morning of 20 May, German gliders and parachutists dropped on the west of the island, around Malme airfield and Chania, both crucial to the Germans for reinforcements. By the end of the day the airfield and the city were still in Allied hands and German casualties were mounting.

German Victory

Overnight the Royal Navy intercepted German and Italian shipping en route to the island. By morning the British fleet had been driven off by the Luftwaffe. Despite heavy pressure, German troops secured Malme and reinforcements poured in, allowing the capture of Chania and the anchorage of Suda Bay. The Germans now pushed along the north coast to the capital, Heraklion, and the remnants of the Allies fought their way to Sphakia on the south coast for evacuation. Of the 22,000 Germans committed to Operation Merkur, 6,000 had been lost. Allied strength, in excess of 41,000 had dwindled to the 15,000 that had been evacuated to Egypt.

24 May: Sinking of the HMS Hood

During the pursuit of the German ships *Bismark* and *Prinz Eugen* the *Hood* and the *Prince of Wales* engaged the enemy ships at a distance of 27 km (17 miles) to the east of Iceland. After an exchange of fire, a shell from the *Bismark* penetrated the *Hood*'s superstructure and exploded in the ammunition lockers. The *Hood* sank in minutes, claiming all but three of the 1,419-man crew. The *Prince of Wales* was also hit and prudently decided to withdraw, while the two German vessels broke away and sailed south.

see Sinking of the HMS Ark Royal p. 94

Sinking of the Bismark

It was not until 26 May that the *Bismark* and *Prinz Eugen*, having sunk the *Hood*, were found again, 1,126 km (700 miles) west of Brest. At 19:50 torpedoes from aircraft of the *Ark Royal* crippled the *Bismark* and the British surface fleet closed in for the kill. At 10:40 on 27 May, after being pulverized by the British fleet, the *Bismark* capsized and sank; only 110 of its crew of 2,300 men survived.

The famous German battleship *Bismark* sinks.

JUNE

The likelihood of the US entering the war came ever closer as Roosevelt froze German and Italian assets and closed the German embassy. In North Africa, the Allies failed to relieve besieged Tobruk, and Hitler's plan to invade Malta was put on hold while Rommel invaded Egypt. A massive German force also invaded Russia, prompting the Finns to try and recapture territory lost during the Winter War.

14 June: Roosevelt Orders the Freezing of German Assets

Continuing pressure on the Axis powers without making an outright commitment to war, Roosevelt froze all German and Italian assets in the United States on 14 June. Two days later the President closed the German Embassy and propaganda offices in the US. In retaliation, on 19 June, Germany and Italy asked the US to close their consulates in their respective countries. On 4 July Roosevelt told the nation that the US was heading for war.

› see US and Britain Warn Japan p. 86

15 June: Operation Battleaxe Fails to Relieve Tobruk

Operation Battleaxe sought to reduce the pressure on Tobruk and relieve the fortress. Initially the British attacks were successful, but by the evening of 15 June German artillery fire had wreaked havoc on the Allied tanks. Rommel responded aggressively and launched counterattacks on the British and to avoid being cut off, the Allied troops retired to the Libyan-Egyptian border. Operation Battleaxe was over in just two days, prompting Churchill to replace Wavell with Auchinleck.

› see Operation Crusader p. 95

21 June: Invasion of Malta Planned

In discussions with Hitler on 21 June 1941, Mussolini agreed to postpone Operation Hercules, the planned invasion of Malta. He agreed to support Rommel's invasion of Egypt before tackling Malta. The proposal was to land three Italian parachute battalions and a German parachute division on Malta, supported by German and Italian aircraft. It was felt that the capture of the strategic point in the Mediterranean would disrupt convoys heading for North Africa.

see Malta VC p. 114

22 June: Germany Invades the Soviet Union

At approximately 04:00 on 22 June, the lead elements of over 100 German divisions began crossing into Russian-held territory. The total German strength amounted to almost 3.2 million men and 3,580 tanks. Around 2.5 million Russians would face them. The Germans advanced on five fronts, from the Baltic to the Black Sea. The opposition they met was ineffective and they were soon deep in Russian territory, having surrounded tens of thousands of Russian troops.

see Germans Drive East p. 83

German tanks enter Russia.

SS Begins Mass Murders

Much of the implementation of the Final Solution was carried out by the organization known as Einsatzgruppen, but the extermination-camp structure and management was overseen by members of the SS. The concentration camps were also used to provide slave labour for SS economic enterprises. Many of the concentration camps had come under the direct jurisdiction of the SS by the middle of 1941, as had the extermination camps. By the end of 1941 concentration camps contained 60,000 prisoners but from 1942 the increased numbers being sent to the camps and the sizes of the camps themselves grew enormously. By January 1945 the SS registered the figure of 741,211 in the concentration camps alone. The SS dictated every action in all the camps which had to be followed.

» see Goerring Presents the Final Solution p. 85

25 June 1941–4 September 1944: Second Finnish-Soviet War

Following the German invasion of Russia, the Finns aimed to recapture the areas they had lost during the Winter War. This period was known to the Finns as the War of Continuation; from 25 June they sought to take up more favourable defensive positions and refused to co-operate with the Germans on the attacks on Leningrad. Border skirmishing continued through to the summer of 1944, by which time it had become clear that Germany was losing the war. The Russians attempted to level Helsinki in February 1944 by bombing, but launched their ground attack on 9 June. They penetrated the Finnish

Finnish troops shelter behind smoking debris on the Karelian Front.

defences the following day and the Finns retreated back to a second line of defence. A large battle took place in the Tali-Ihantala area (25 June–6 July), but Russian losses caused them to break off the attack. Meanwhile, other major Russian assaults continued until 11 July. The ceasefire was officially signed at 07:00 on 4 September 1944. The Russians only retained the area they had won during the Winter War. Finland had maintained its independence and much of its territorial integrity.

see Winter War p. 28

28 June: Germans Drive East

With German troops threatening Minsk and closing on Kiev towards the end of June 1940, the Russian army was either in full retreat or had already been cut off. By 9 July the Russians had lost over 300,000 men and 2,500 tanks; in the Bialystok sector, 40 divisions had been wiped out. German units began moving towards Smolensk, en route for Moscow. Elsewhere, the Germans and their allies were advancing on a broad front.

see Stalin Begins a Scorched-Earth Policy p. 84

German tanks advancing across Russia.

JULY

Following the German invasion of Russia, Stalin advocated a scorched-earth policy and called up all men aged between 16 and 60. The German occupation of the country continued, with the Luftwaffe bombing Moscow in mid-July. Japanese assets in Britain and the US were frozen following Japan's occupation of French Indo-China. In Germany, Goering presented the Final Solution, the Nazis' response to the 'Jewish problem'.

3 July: Stalin Begins a Scorched-Earth Policy

On 3 July, for the first time since the invasion, Stalin addressed the Russian people, admitting vast losses of men and territory. He urged the Russians to resist until the bitter end and leave nothing for the Germans. He advocated a scorched-earth policy, in which everything of value that had to be left behind would be destroyed. All men between the ages of 16 and 60 were called up and given orders to defend positions to the last man at all costs.

» see Joseph Stalin p. 242

14 July–29 August: British Occupy Syria and Enter Iran with Soviets

In Syria an armistice was signed between the British and the French and Syria was declared independent. On 15 July British troops entered Beirut and Syria and Lebanon came under Allied control. On 26 August British troops occupied the oil fields at Abadan in Iran and the following day a new government was formed, allowing British and Russian troops to be stationed around the country.

British prisoners-of-war being returned after the occupation of Syria in 1941.

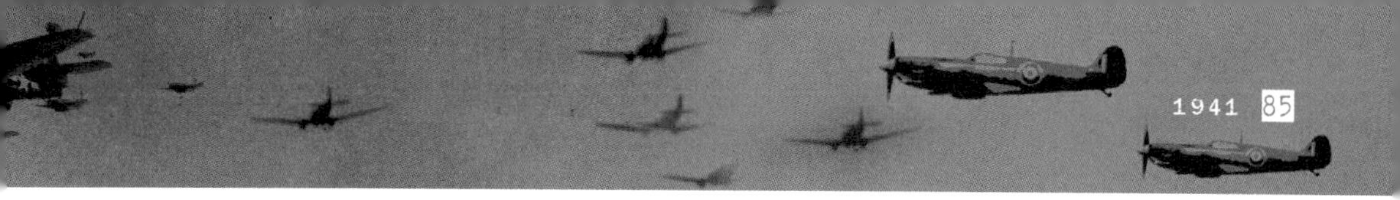

17 July: Germans Cross the Dniepr

The Germans established a bridgehead on the River Dniepr, east of Minsk, on 17 July. By 27 July Smolensk was surrounded; more than 700,000 Russians had been trapped and 300,000 were taken prisoner along with 3,000 tanks and 1,000 aircraft.

› see Germans Capture Novgorod p. 87

21 July: Luftwaffe Bombs Moscow

With German troops continuing to advance on all fronts, Moscow fell within enemy reach. On the night of 21 July, massive night air attacks rained bombs on the Russian capital. Each day thousands more Russian troops fell into German hands as town after town was overrun. The Germans bombed Moscow again on 3 August and over 300,000 Russians surrendered near Smolensk two days later.

› see Hermann Goering p. 231

24 July: Japanese Occupy French Indo-China

Japanese forces began occupying French-held Indo-China on 24 July. Officially they collaborated with the French forces in its defence. The next day Japanese assets in Britain and the US were frozen; Japan reciprocated and Canada also froze their trade with Japan. By 29 July the Japanese occupation of Indo-China was complete. Britain sent reinforcements to Singapore on 6 August.

› see Tojo Replaces Konoye as Prime Minister of Japan p. 90

31 July: Goering Presents The Final Solution

Much of the organization and planning regarding the German's 'Jewish problem' had been left to Adolf Eichmann, who had been placed in charge of Jewish emigration. In 1941 he was appointed Head of the Gestapo, the department responsible for the 'Final Solution'. Goering signed Eichmann's draft and charged Heydrich with the task of 'evacuating' all European Jews. The wording of the agreement was ambiguous, but everyone around the conference table knew what these carefully couched terms meant. Eichmann was interned by US troops in 1945, but escaped to South America. The Israelis discovered him in Argentina and he was hanged in May 1962.

› see Jews Ordered to Wear Yellow Stars p. 87

AUGUST AND SEPTEMBER

Churchill and Roosevelt discussed war aims at the Atlantic Conference, resulting in the Atlantic Charter. German territorial gains in Russia increased, and they grew ever nearer to Leningrad. September was the month that all Jews were ordered to wear the yellow star for identification; special German squads murdered thousands of Jews in Kiev. As the Germans eventually surrounded Leningrad, the long siege of the city began.

6 August: US and Britain Warn Japan

On 26 July Roosevelt froze Japanese assets in the US, suspended trade and set an oil embargo. On 6 August, along with the British, he warned the Japanese not to invade Thailand. Japan responded by stating it had no aggressive intentions. On 8 August the Japanese Ambassador to Washington proposed talks between Roosevelt and the Japanese Prime Minister to sort out differences between their countries.

Japanese war planes

9–12 August: Atlantic Charter

On 9 August British Prime Minister Churchill and US President Roosevelt met in Placentia Bay in Newfoundland and the following day opened the Atlantic Conference. The result of this conference – the Atlantic Charter – would define the war aims. Churchill wanted the US to enter the war, but Roosevelt refused to make any guarantee of this. Neither Roosevelt nor Churchill was under any illusions about Japanese intentions and they proposed to force the Japanese to accept that Thailand and French Indo-China should be neutral. Other issues were discussed and the conference broke up on 12 August.

see Creation of the United Nations p. 104

17 August: Germans Capture Novgorod

In the northern sector of the Eastern Front, the Germans to the south-east of the key Russian city of Leningrad captured Novgorod on 17 August. In the south they took Dniepr and threatened Kharkov; the Crimea and Odessa were also surrounded. By 22 August the Russians had lost 1.25 million men, 14,000 tanks, 15,000 guns and over 11,000 aircraft. Between 24 and 26 August limited Russian counterattacks were defeated.

September: Jews Ordered to Wear Yellow Stars

The compulsory wearing of a yellow star to indicate that an individual was Jewish began in September, in occupied Eastern Europe. The system was extended to the rest of the Third Reich territories shortly afterwards and all Jews over the age of six were obliged to wear one. The star had to be worn on the left side of all outer garments and was permanently stitched so that it could not easily be removed. The order was just another step in the Nazi Final Solution.

see Germans Murder 30,000 Jews at Kiev p. 89

1 September: Leningrad is Surrounded

German troops reached the southern shore of Lake Ladoga on 1 September, cutting off the key city of Leningrad from the rest of Russia. The Germans also established bridgeheads on the Gulf of Finland. For 90 days German troops launched a series of offensives all driving

towards the capture of Leningrad. Although the situation was desperate for the Russians, in an act of courageous defiance, Zhukov ordered the city to be fortified – house by house, street by street – to deny the Germans their prize.

8 September–27 January 1944: Siege of Leningrad

The Siege of Leningrad officially began on 8 September 1941; it lasted until 27 January 1944, making it the longest siege in the war. Nearly three million Russian civilians were trapped in the city for the duration of the siege. Food and fuel were in limited supply and by the winter of 1941 there was no heating or water. By January 1942 daily rations had dropped to just 125 g of bread per day and from January to February an estimated 200,000 people died of starvation or the cold alone. Despite the hardships, however, the people of Leningrad held out with remarkable tenacity.

The Siege of Leningrad.

Lifting of Siege

The siege was officially broken in January 1943, but it was not for another year that it was fully lifted. By this time between 650,000 and 800,000 Leningrad citizens and soldiers had been killed. Some half a million of these are buried in the Piskariovskoye Memorial Cemetery.

Restoration of Leningrad

The Russians made it a national task to restore Leningrad to its former glory after the many months of constant bombardment. War damage had affected virtually every building, yet Leningrad – now called St Petersburg – was successfully restored and museums and public buildings reopened.

➧ see Germans Capture Kharkov and Kursk p. 90

11 September: Roosevelt Orders a 'Shoot-First' Policy

On 4 September the USS *Greer* was attacked by a German U-boat in the waters south-west of Iceland. Roosevelt was furious and on 11 September ordered a 'shoot-first' policy to all US ships encountering either German or Italian vessels. Any ship that threatened the passage of US merchant ships or their escorts would henceforth come under attack from the US navy. The policy was to take immediate effect.

➧ see Sinking of the USS Reuben James p. 90

28–29 September: Germans Murder 30,000 Jews at Kiev

German Special Operations squads, known as 'Einsatzgruppen', entered both Poland and Russia behind the advancing German armies with the specific purpose of rounding up and killing Jews. At Kiev, in a ravine known as Babi Yar to the north-west, 30,000 Jews were murdered in just two days. Many had been turned in by local Ukrainians.

➧ see First Jews Gassed p. 99

OCTOBER

Tojo was elected as the new Japanese prime minister, prompting his country's entrance into war against the Allies and the US. By late October, the German army was closing in on Moscow, and German U-boats sunk the USS *Reuben James*, the first American vessel lost to hostile action.

17 October: Tojo Replaces Konoye as Prime Minister of Japan

Tojo symbolized the pro-war faction in Japan; it would be at his insistence that Japan went to war against the Allies and, significantly, the US. As a politician, he refused to meddle in operational matters, but was a capable bureaucrat more than able to carry out the Japanese Imperial Cabinet's wishes. Tojo accepted responsibility for Japanese reversals and when Saipan was lost in July 1944 he resigned, blaming himself.

see Hideki Tojo p. 244

24 October–3 November: Germans Capture Kharkov and Kursk

By 20 October, the Germans were within 105 km (65 miles) of Moscow. Three days later two German armies were closing in on Kharkov. As bad weather began to hinder the offensive against Moscow, Kharkov was taken on 24 October. After seizing most of the Crimea in the south, the Germans captured Kursk to the north of Kharkov on 3 November before continuing their march on Moscow.

see Assault on Moscow p. 95

31 October: Sinking of the USS Reuben James

The USS *Reuben James* was part of an escort force protecting shipping bound for Britain, one of five destroyers assigned to convoy HX-156. Early on 31 October, it was torpedoed by the U-Boat U-522. The torpedo hit the ship's magazine and it sank in minutes, claiming 100 of the crew and becoming the first US vessel lost to hostile action.

see Allies Declare War on Japan p. 98

1931–45: War in China

The Japanese invaded north-eastern China in 1931. Over the 15 years of war that ensued, some 30 million Chinese would be killed. Japanese policy seemed to revolve around mass reprisal killings, slave labour and other violent indignities against the civilian population. The infamous Rape of Nanking lasted six weeks and claimed over 300,000 lives. During the war, US and British forces supported and supplied the Chinese. Ultimately, however, the war sapped the strength of the nationalist government and was a contributing factor in the Communist victory in 1949.

Japanese tanks breach a ford in China.

1941–45: Flying Tigers

The volunteer group Flying Tigers was created by former US Army Air Corps Colonel, Claire L. Chennault, to replace Russia's support of China against Japan. By 1941, as Air Advisor to the Chinese nationalist government, he had purchased 100 Curtiss Tomahawks and attracted over 100 pilots on one-year contracts. Three squadrons flew the distinctive shark-tooth marked planes, making their first attack on Japanese aircraft on 20 December 1941. From their formation to the end of hostilities they claimed 621 enemy aircraft shot down, with 320 destroyed on the ground.

see Chiang Kai-shek p. 228

The insignia for the volunteer group the Flying Tigers.

NOVEMBER

In Yugoslavia, civil war broke out between the two opposing factions, the Chetniks and Tito's Communists. The former collaborated with the Germans, while the latter received aid and assistance from Britain. In Britain itself, the air offensive against Germany was stepped up. Operation Crusader was launched to reinforce Tobruk, and this time the British were successful against Rommel's forces. Meanwhile, German troops drew ever closer to Moscow.

2 November: Chetniks Battle with Tito

By November it was apparent that the Chetniks and Tito's Communists would never see eye to eye, either on the way in which to deal with the occupying forces or on the future of Yugoslavia. A civil war broke out between the two groups. Mihailovic met with the Germans on 11 November, to begin his collaboration with them.

1941–45: Tito's Partisans

Following the German invasion of Yugoslavia, Croatia was made an independent state, the Italians occupied parts of Slovenia, Montenegro, Kosovo and areas along the Dalmatian Coast. Bulgaria annexed Macedonia and the majority of Serbia, and eastern Slovenia was annexed by Germany. Two resistance organizations emerged: the Communists under Tito and the Serb royalist Chetniks. To begin with, both partisan groups resisted occupation and in January 1943 the Germans and the Italians attempted to wipe out Partisan activity in a major offensive.

Holding Fast

A good grasp of tactics and difficult terrain saved Tito's men, who were on the ascendancy in terms of support. The Germans continued to battle with Tito's Partisans, who were by now well supplied with captured equipment and were receiving additional assistance from British aircraft, which flew in supplies and advisors. The Germans continued to try to wipe out Tito's men until 1944, when they began their retreat from the Balkans. Tito was able to take Belgrade just hours before the Russian army arrived. His men participated in the capture of Zagreb on 9 May 1945.

Post-war Divide

Although pro-Soviet, post-war Yugoslavia found itself in the British-dominated zone of Europe, along with Greece and Albania.

see Germans Attempt to Snatch Tito p. 160

1939–45: 'The Sea Shall Not Have Them'

The vital task of recovering downed aircraft crews from the oceans grew increasingly important throughout the war. Apart from the moral obligation to rescue the men there was also the practical issue of having to replace experienced crew. The RAF Marine Craft section originated during World War I, and the RAF developed the service during the 1930s. By the outbreak of the war it had a network of launches and flying boats capable of going out in all weathers to search for ditched crews. It is estimated that at least 14,000 men owed their lives to the RAF alone. Similar services had been set up by Australia and were active in the Pacific. Wherever British aircraft were posted, an RAF Marine Craft section unit was sent to deal with air-sea rescue. Shortly after the war the service was incorporated fully into the RAF and ultimately the helicopter took over many of the duties.

see Thousand-Bomber Raid p. 117

Survivors from the HMS *Ark Royal*.

7 November: British Launch their Largest Air Operation

Under continual pressure to step up its air offensive against Germany, Bomber Command launched nearly 400 aircraft against Berlin, Cologne and Manheim. To date this was the heaviest RAF offensive of the war. The flight to Berlin of 1,700 km (1,056 miles) succeeded in catching the Germans unaware, but at least 37 aircraft were lost as a result of poor weather conditions. The British had been routinely bombing German targets with increasing effect, but had needed to split their assets to deal with Italian targets around the Mediterranean. Their aim was the prevention of Italian and German reinforcements arriving in North Africa.

see Bomber Command p. 73

14 November: Sinking of the HMS Ark Royal

Early on 14 November, just off the coast of Gibraltar, the HMS *Ark Royal* fell victim to an Italian submarine attack. The majority of the crew was saved. The vessel had been a continual thorn in the German and Italian sides since the beginning of the war and both countries had claimed to have sunk the ship in the past. The aircraft carrier slipped beneath the waters at around 06:00.

see Japanese Capture Hong Kong p. 101

The HMS *Ark Royal* sinks beneath the waves.

18–28 November: Operation Crusader

General Cunningham's 8th Army launched Operation Crusader in order to reinforce Tobruk. After initial successes, both the Italians and the Germans began to put up a stiff fight. In a major attack towards Tobruk, one British armoured brigade lost 113 of its 141 tanks. The Tobruk garrison managed to break out and join the 8th Army on 28 November and by the beginning of December the British had achieved a strategic success in North Africa. On 2 December Rommel launched a final attack against Tobruk, but could make no headway. Within a week, the supply corridor to Tobruk had been re-established by the British.

21 November: Assault on Moscow

The Germans seized Rostov by a frontal attack. The occupation was completed by 21 November, by which time lead German units had reached Istra, 30 miles to the north-west of Moscow. The Donetz industrial and mineral areas were now under German control. In appalling weather, the German advance began to slow and the Russians planned a series of counteroffensives.

see Germans Abandon the Attack on Moscow p. 96

The road to Moscow.

DECEMBER

This was one of the most dramatic months of the war to date. The British campaign to reopen the Burma Road moved up a gear. Germany abandoned its attack on Moscow and the first Jews were gassed at Chelmno. The main story, however, was the Japanese attack on the US naval base in Pearl Harbor. It catapulted the US into the war, and was a major turning point in the whole conflict.

December 1941–August 1945: Burma Campaign

One of the main reasons for the campaign in Burma was the need to maintain an overland supply route to China. In the early months, the war was a disaster for the British: they were outmanoeuvred, outfought and forced to retreat from Burma to the comparative safety of India. The chief units during the war were from the Indian Army, but Ghurkas, East and West Africans, other local ethnic groups, Americans, Canadians and Chinese would all participate against the Japanese invaders.

The Burma Road

After the Japanese later overran Burma in 1942, the principle struggle was to reopen the Burma Road and, meanwhile, transport and supply troops by air. Jungle airstrips needed to be cut and the area's many rivers needed to be patrolled and denied to the enemy. Had the Japanese been able to penetrate into India, any hope of displacing them would have been lost, so, often against great odds, scratch Allied units fought desperate actions in extremely difficult conditions.

➧ see Japanese Invade Burma p. 106

5 December: Germans Abandon their Attack on Moscow

Reserves amounting to over 100 divisions and supported by 1,500 tanks, launched a counteroffensive against the 67 German divisions menacing Moscow on 5 December. The

Germans were taken by surprise and the Russians penetrated German lines to a depth of 18 km (11 miles). The Russians continued offensive actions throughout December, but no major territory was lost. For the first time German casualties were mounting.

see Germans Capture Sevastopol p. 122

7 December: Pearl Harbor

On 27 March 1941, the Japanese spy Takeo Yoshikawa arrived in Hawaii to study the US naval fleet, which had its base at Pearl Harbor on the island. His information provided the intelligence the Japanese needed to launch the pre-emptive attack on 7 December that took the US completely by surprise. The Japanese deployed six aircraft carriers and over 400 aircraft in the attacks, which killed 2,400 US personnel and accounted for 18 US vessels either sunk or badly damaged. The Japanese's primary target had been the US aircraft carriers, which were on manoeuvres at the time; the US Navy were able to use these carriers and submarines to first stop and then reverse Japanese fortunes in the Pacific.

The US fleet is attacked at anchor at the Hawaiian base Pearl Harbor.

A Turning Point

The Japanese missed the opportunity to destroy the vast oil reserves held at Pearl Harbor, which would have taken months to replace and would have prevented the US fleet from taking any offensive actions. However, the attack on Pearl Harbor was a serious blow to the US, not just practically, but also in terms of morale. Nevertheless, by 1945, only one of the twenty two Japanese ships that took part in the Pearl Harbor operation would still be afloat. In the longer-term, the attack was a turning point in the war, assuaging any doubts the US had about joining the conflict.

see Allies Declare War on Japan p. 98

Japanese Fighter Bombers

The Japanese developed a range of fighter bombers, most of which were capable of taking off from aircraft carriers or from land-based airstrips. Some were adapted primarily to deliver torpedoes, such as the Kate and the Jill. Others were designed to deliver a single bomb, such as the Val, Nell and Betty. The Kates were responsible for the sinking of three American aircraft carriers within the first 12 months of the war. By 1944 the Kate was obsolete; however 1,149 were built between 1936 and 1943.

Japanese bombers.

8 December: Allies Declare War on Japan

In the aftermath of the Japanese attack on the naval base at Pearl Harbor, the United States and Britain declared war on the empire of Japan. On the same day the Japanese invaded the Philippines, Malaya and Hong Kong. On 10 December Japanese units landed on Guam to begin occupation. The Japanese had also landed at Bataan without opposition and the American garrisons in Shanghai and Tientsin in China were captured.

see Germany and Italy Declare War on the US p. 100

8 December: Japan Invades Siam and Malaysia

Early on 8 December, Japanese bombers began attacks on Singapore. Fearful of a Japanese invasion, HMS *Prince of Wales* and HMS *Repulse* were sent to intercept the Japanese invasion fleet. The Japanese had already landed at Khota Bharu on the east coast of Malaya, near the Thai border, and at Singora in Thailand itself. At this point all the British could do was carry out a reconnaissance.

see Japanese Capture Hong Kong p. 101

8 December: First Jews Gassed

The Nazi concentration camp at Chelmno, which dealt with Jews from the Lodz ghetto, was the first fully functional extermination camp. Using mobile gas vans it claimed its first victims on 8 December. It has been estimated that around 700,000 Jews were killed in these vans, but the system had been tested on mentally ill Polish children. The Polish city of Lodz had a Jewish population of 223,000 before the Germans arrived; by 1945 there were just 6,000 left in the ghetto.

see Gassing Begins at Auschwitz p. 104

10 December: Sinking of the Prince of Wales and the Repulse

After leaving Singapore to intercept a Japanese invasion fleet, on 9 December the two British vessels were spotted by a Japanese submarine. Fortunately the captain gave the wrong coordinates and Japanese torpedo-carrying aircraft could not find either vessel. The following day, however, the Japanese found their targets and the *Prince of Wales* and *Repulse* were sunk by torpedoes and bombs. The *Prince of Wales* had been part of the fleet that accounted for the *Bismark*. It had also been the venue for the meeting between Roosevelt and Churchill in August 1941.

10 December: Japanese land at Luzon

Bangkok, the Thai capital, fell on 9 December and the following day Japanese troops landed at Luzon in the Philippines. The Americans resisted but were hopelessly outnumbered and faced powerful Japanese air support, which claimed a US destroyer and two submarines.

➧ see Japanese Capture Hong Kong p. 101

11 December: Germany and Italy Declare War on the US

Hitler, in the Reichstag, and Mussolini, speaking from the balcony of the Palazzo Venezia, declared war on the US on 11 December. The US reciprocated in kind. In the House of Commons Churchill noted 'In Hitler's launching of the Nazi campaign on Russia we can already see, after less than six months of fighting, that he has made one of the outstanding blunders of history.'

14 December: Convoy HG76

HG76 is seen as the beginning of the military strategy that led to the decisive convoy battle of early 1943 and the defeat of the U-boats. HG76 sailed from Gibraltar on 15 December expecting a difficult voyage. For the first time, the Royal Navy destroyed a wolf pack of U-boats. The new escort tactics and information from the cracked German naval code led, between 17 and 21 December, to the sinking of four of the nine U-boats attacking the convoy outside Gibraltar.

➧ see Wolf Packs p. 26

20 December: Japanese Invade Mindanao and Wake Island

The Japanese landed on Davao on the island of Mindanao on 20 December. The following day some 43,000 Japanese troops arrived to the north of Manila in the Gulf of Lingayen. On 22 December further Japanese landings took place at Bauang, Aringay and Agoo. That night Japanese troops began landing on Wake Island. The struggle for the Philippines was reaching its climax.

The battle of Wake Island.

Wake Island

On the morning of 22 December, the Japanese invasion fleet arrived off Wake Island, a small, v-shaped rock, 4,000 km (2,500 miles) west of Pearl Harbor. The first defence battalion could only muster around 385 men, but in the event the Japanese were only able to land on the adjacent Wilkes Island. The sheer weight of numbers and dwindling defenders meant that the Japanese took just 45 minutes to overrun the garrison once they arrived there. The defence troops had held out for 15 days and a quarter of their number had been killed or wounded. The defenders would spend three years in Japanese prisoner of war camps. Wake Island was liberated by US troops on 14 May 1944.

» see Japanese Take Manila p. 104

25 December: Japanese Capture Hong Kong

Japanese troops began their attack on Hong Kong on 18 December and within 24 hours they were able to occupy half of the area. By 25 December the British garrison had been under siege for seven days. At 09:00 they proposed their surrender terms and that afternoon the British commander gave the order to surrender. Many local Chinese welcomed the Japanese troops, waving Japanese flags.

1942

JANUARY

The New Year saw the creation of the United Nations. The Japanese campaign continued unabated with the invasion of Manila, Kuala Lumpur, Burma and the Solomon Islands. It was likely that gassing began at Auschwitz also this month, and the Wannsee Conference was held to organize the coordination of the Final Solution.

January: Gassing Begins at Auschwitz

The two associated camps at Auschwitz had carried out experimental gassing on Russian prisoners of war around September 1941 and it is likely that the system started at Auschwitz itself in January 1942. Systems were set up to deal with 6,000 people per day. Transports arrived from Poland, Slovakia, the Netherlands, Belgium and Yugoslavia. By January 1943 the first transports were arriving from Berlin and by May 1944 Hungarian Jews were arriving. At least 20,000 gypsies were also liquidated and their bodies burned. Auschwitz became the largest graveyard in Europe, where almost a quarter of all murdered met their end.

➧ see Heydrich is Attacked in Prague p. 117

1 January: Creation of the United Nations

By 1 January 1942, 26 nations, including the US, Great Britain, Russia, China, Greece, Norway and Yugoslavia, had signed the Atlantic Charter. In effect this was the creation of the United Nations. They were to 'Ensure life, liberty, independence and religious freedom and to preserve the rights of man and justice.' The 26 were implacably opposed to the Axis doctrine and purposes.

➧ see Stalin and Churchill Meet in Moscow p. 127

2 January: Japanese Take Manila

US and Filipino forces evacuated the area north of Manila on 2 January 1942, allowing the Japanese to consolidate their control of the Philippine capital. The US troops retreated towards the Bataan peninsula under constant attack. By 7 January the Japanese had forced all remaining US and Filipino units into the Bataan peninsula; they then proceeded towards the coast.

A6M Zero (1939–45)

The Zero, codenamed 'Zeke' by the Allies, was the most famous Japanese aircraft of the war. The first of 11,000 aircraft, designed and built by Mitsubishi, flew on 1 April 1939. It was small and highly manoeuvrable with a maximum speed of around 500 kph (311 mph). However, as pilot losses mounted and US aircraft became more deadly, the Zero was no longer the force it had once been. Attempts were made to improve the performance, but after 1943 it could no longer compete. A newer version in 1945 came close, but by this stage it was too late to deal with the hundreds of US aircraft dominating the skies.

A Zero (A6M).

10 January: Japanese Capture Kuala Lumpur

The Indian 3rd Corps attempted to hold a line against the Japanese between 8 and 9 January but the following day the British ordered the abandonment of Kuala Lumpur, which was immediately occupied by the Japanese. The Indian corps continued its retreat southward, under heavy Japanese air attack. On 13 January additional British reinforcements arrived in Singapore and were deployed across the Malayan peninsular to hold off the Japanese attacks.

➧ see Japan Invades Siam and Malaysia p. 99

11 January: Operation Paukenschlag

Operation Paukenschlag ('Drumbeat') was a German campaign carried out along the east coast of the United States. U-boats had been intercepting British convoys around Newfoundland and it was now proposed to attack the US coastline from New York to Florida. Five U-boats began their attacks on 11 January, claiming their first victim the following day. The operation ended on 6 February, having claimed 25 merchant ships and 156,939 tons of war materials.

➧ see Wolf Packs p. 26

16 January: Japanese Invade Burma

Japanese forces began their offensive in Burma by attacking Myitta and Tavoy on 16 January. Within three days Japanese troops were attacking in the Moulmein area and by 23 January they had achieved air superiority and were threatening Rangoon. There was a lull towards the end of the month as they began reorganizing for a new push. On 30 January the Japanese captured the airport at Moulmein and the following day began to shell Martaban.

➧ see Burma Campaign p. 96

Japanese enter Rangoon.

20 January: Wannsee Conference

This meeting aimed to deal with the bureaucratic coordination of the slaughter of 11 million Jews in Europe. The conference not only identified the exact numbers and locations of all Jews in German territory, but also laid down the treatment and definition of a Jew. Those who matched certain criteria with regard to mixed blood would be sterilized, all others would be eliminated. Some 537,000 Jews had already left German-controlled Europe by the end of October 1941. Since then all emigration had been prohibited. Already hundreds of thousands, primarily those in Russia, had been killed.

➧ see Goering Presents the Final Solution p. 85

21 January–1 July: Renewed German Offensive and Gazala Line

Rommel launched a major offensive towards Agedabia on 21 January. The Axis troops advanced eastward, managing to outflank the prepared British defences. The British began to retire and by 25 January were on the road to Benghazi. By 1 July the British had been rolled all the way back into Egypt. This would be the high watermark of German successes in North Africa; soon it would be Rommel being chased across North Africa.

➧ see Erwin Rommel p. 241

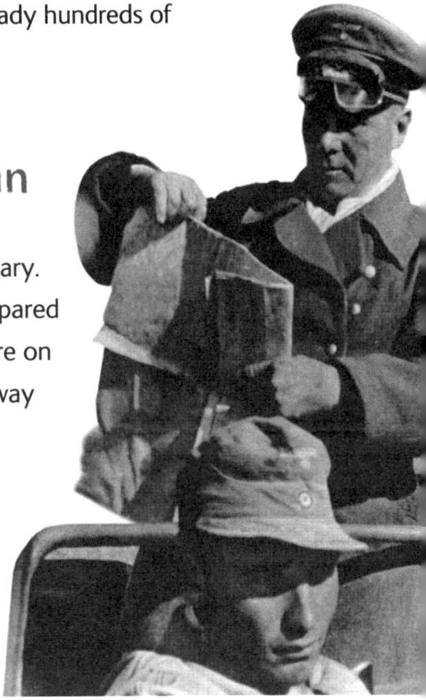

Erwin Rommel.

23 January: Japanese Land in the Solomons

Japanese troops began landing on New Guinea and Bougainville in the Solomon Islands on 23 January; they met very little opposition. In New Guinea Allied troops evacuated the capital, Lae, and Salamaua on 24 January, just a day before the Japanese landed. By 28 January they had taken Rossel Island, east of New Guinea, and were dangerously close to Australia. On 2 February the Japanese began to menace Port Moresby, the capital of Papua.

➧ see Japanese Capture Borneo Oilfields p. 108

FEBRUARY

The Japanese domination of the Far East progressed with the invasion of Borneo, parts of Indonesia, and the capture and fall of Singapore. In an attempt to prevent a full-scale invasion of Java, the Allies intercepted the Japanese in the Java Sea, but suffered a disastrous defeat.

6 February: Japanese Capture Borneo Oilfields

The Japanese took Samarinda, off the east coast of Borneo on 6 February, and by 10 February their occupation of Borneo and Celebes was well underway. On 13 February they occupied Banjermasin and on the following day Japanese paratroops landed in Sumatra, forcing the Dutch garrison to retire. On 15 February the Japanese invasion fleet arrived off Sumatra and Allied troops headed for Java. Within four days the Japanese had invaded Bali.

15 February: Fall of Singapore

Despite General Percival's defiance that Singapore would not fall while an Allied soldier still stood, on 8 February at 08:45, two Japanese divisions landed on the north-west coast. They were able to establish a bridgehead and Percival sent reinforcements the following day, but 15,000 Japanese troops managed to cross the waters between the Malayan mainland and the island of Singapore. In response the British withdrew from the west of the island and on 10 February they established a defence line. The subsequent counterattack was a failure.

Unconditional Surrender

On 11 February General Yamashita ordered that leaflets be dropped on Singapore, asking the island to surrender. When this demand was ignored Japanese troops attacked along the whole of the Allied perimeter, forcing all Allied shipping to evacuate the harbour. The

Japanese continued their attacks and with ammunition, food and water running out, Percival signed an unconditional surrender at 19:50 on 15 February. The Gibraltar of the east had fallen.

22 February: MacArthur is Ordered to Leave Bataan

Under strict orders from President Roosevelt himself, General MacArthur left the Philippines on 22 February, uttering promises to return. MacArthur transferred his headquarters to Australia. On 26 February a large Japanese amphibious invasion fleet left Luzon for Mindoro; if it fell, US troops based in Bataan would be completely cut off. On 1 March an advanced party of Japanese landed at Zamboango on Mindanao.

see Douglas MacArthur p. 236

US commander General Douglas MacArthur.

27 February–1 March: Battle of the Java Sea

In an attempt to prevent the invasion of Java, an Allied task force intercepted the Japanese near Surabaya. The squadron of five cruisers and 11 destroyers suffered heavy casualties: three were sunk, two were badly damaged and the rest were incapable of further offensive actions. They landed the following day, encountering little opposition. By 3 March Japanese forces were close enough to Australia to begin air raids.

see Japanese Capture Java p. 110

MARCH

General Alexander was appointed commander of Allied forces in Burma, but he was powerless to halt the Japanese entering Rangoon and ordered an immediate evacuation. The Allies' failure to protect Java left the way open for the Japanese to take the island. Allied commando units destroyed the St Nazaire dry dock, putting it out of action for the rest of the war.

5 March: Alexander is Appointed Commander in Burma

In early March, General Alexander replaced General Wavell as commander of Allied forces in Burma. Wavell had already given orders that Allied troops would withdraw from Rangoon and Alexander immediately ordered counterattacks in order to relieve Pegu and to close the gap between the 17th Indian Division and the 1st Burmese Division. Rangoon was evacuated on 7 March and the Japanese 33rd Division marched into the city.

see Harold Alexander p. 226

British commander Harold Alexander.

7 March: Japanese Capture Java

By 1 March, with the Allied fleet badly mauled and Allied aircraft destroyed, the Japanese spread out across Java, while Allied ships headed for Australia. On 2 March the Japanese captured the capital, Batavia, and the Dutch were forced to fall back, destroying everything that they left behind them. Finally, on 7 March, Java fell to the Japanese. The Dutch government had fled to Australia and what remained of the garrisons surrendered to the Japanese.

see Japanese Capture Bataan p. 112

8 March: Japanese Take Rangoon

On 5 March Alexander arrived in Rangoon and took command of all troops in Burma. He ordered an immediate counteroffensive but the Japanese had already attacked Pegu and cut off the road to Rangoon. Alexander, now aware of the severity of the situation, ordered Rangoon to be evacuated. The garrison at Pegu was ordered to break out and head north and on 8 March the Japanese entered Rangoon, with Indian infantry managing to break through the Japanese lines in order to allow the Allied troops to retire. The retreat continued and new Allied headquarters were set up near Mandalay.

see The Chindits p. 136

28 March: Raid on St Nazaire

Early on 28 March, Operation Chariot hit home against St Nazaire at the mouth of the Loire River, when HMS *Campbeltown* rammed the dock gates. The port was the Germans' only dry dock on the Atlantic coast, primarily used as a U-boat base. The task force, consisting of a number of motor boats and torpedo boats, in addition to the converted destroyer, carried 200 men from No. 2 Commando, along with demolition teams from eight other Commando units. When the *Campbeltown* hit the dock gates at 20 knots, the Commandos placed charges to destroy German facilities. As they escaped in launches down river, five tons of explosives on board *Campbeltown* put the dry dock out of action for the remainder of the war. A German ship in the estuary tried to stop the escapees, but she was misidentified and sunk by German coastal batteries.

1941–45: Commandos

Commandos were involved in the war for the first time in December 1941, at Vaagso in Norway, then in Dieppe in August 1942. On 6 June 1944 they captured the River Orne bridges, under the command of Lord Lovat. The Commandos are credited with 38 battle honours between 1940 and 1945 and their existence was much favoured by Churchill.

APRIL

April saw more Japanese attacks, notably when the Bataan peninsular in the Philippines was captured. Thousands of prisoners were taken following the invasion, and the notorious Bataan Death March followed during which thousands died. Louis Mountbatten was appointed Chief of Combined Operations. A US bombing raid took place on Tokyo in revenge for the attacks on Pearl Harbor.

2–8 April: Air Assault on Malta

Although Malta had been under attack for nearly four months by April 1942, some of the most vicious raids took place in the first week of that month. On 5 April a British destroyer was sunk and two others were badly damaged in Valletta harbour; on 7 April the island suffered its heaviest attack, its 2,000th of the war. Control of Malta's harbour and airfields were imperative.

see Malta VC p. 114

9 April: Japanese Capture Bataan

On 8 April 1942 the American perimeter on the Bataan peninsular collapsed; 2,000 men managed to escape to Corregidor. At 12:30 on 9 April the unconditional surrender came into effect. During the capture the Japanese had netted 67,000 prisoners; thousands more would die during the Bataan Death March that followed the capture of the city. Within hours of the surrender Corregidor came under artillery fire and the Japanese found themselves free to make an assault on the island of Cebu.

Bataan Death March

The following day, the march north began towards Camp O'Donnell. Any man who faltered was summarily executed by the guards. Of the 9,300 US troops on the march, up to 650 died en route; casualties amongst the Filipinos were higher – of the 45,000 at least 5,000 died. The casualties at Camp O'Donnell were no better: in the first 40 days, some 1,500 US troops died and by the end of July the Filipino death toll had broken 20,000. This forced the Japanese to move the prisoners to a new camp at Cabanatuan, where they were joined by more US prisoners taken at Corregidor.

see Battle of the Coral Sea p. 116

12 April: Mountbatten is Appointed Chief of Combined Operations

Mountbatten managed to jump several ranks when he was named Chief of Combined Operations; with it he claimed a seat on the Chiefs of Staff Committee. He was given senior ranks in the army, navy and air force in order to validate his position. He would oversee a number of Commando operations, including Dieppe and St Nazaire. This was a post he would hold until early 1943.

see Louis Mountbatten p. 238

The Grand Harbour on the island of Malta under air attack.

16 April: Malta VC

On 16 April, after suffering some four months of daily attacks, King George VI awarded the George Cross, the civilian Victoria Cross, to the island of Malta. The King praised the heroism and devotion of its people. Malta represented a constant thorn in Rommel's side and since assuming command in North Africa he had made it a priority to subdue the island. Up until this point very little in the way of supplies had managed to get through to Malta and the island was under continual threat from up to 600 German and Italian aircraft based in Sicily. A handful of Spitfires remained in operation throughout the aerial siege and bombardment. The first Allied convoy made it safely into Malta on 14 August 1942.

see Convoy HG76 p. 100

18 April: Doolittle Raid

After Pearl Harbor, there was an outcry for revenge against the Japanese. On 18 April twenty-four crews were selected from the 17th Bombardment Group. The planes took off from the ocean off the Japanese coast, led by Lieutenant Colonel James H. Doolittle. They launched from USS *Hornet* in modified B-25s – destination Tokyo. They achieved complete surprise when they dropped the first bombs on the Japanese city.

James Doolittle, with the airmen who took part in the raids on Tokyo.

Morale Boost

All but one of the aircraft made it to their landing spot in China; Doolittle bailed out just north of Chuchow and linked up with Chinese guerrillas. He was promoted to Brigadier General and awarded the Medal of Honor. In terms of damage, the raid had been a failure but the purpose was to prove to the American public and the Japanese authorities that Japan was not impervious to attack.

1942: B-25

The North American B-25 Mitchell medium bomber was undoubtedly one of the most famous US aircraft of World War II. It was the aircraft chosen by Doolittle when he raided Tokyo in April 1942; it would see service in virtually every region of combat and in addition to US use it would also be flown by British, Dutch, Australian and Russian pilots. It was primarily designed as a medium-altitude bomber, but it was used extensively against Japanese airfields at low level or for strafing or bombing attacks on Japanese shipping. Nearly 10,000 B-25s were built during the war. The aircraft had a maximum speed of 443 kph (275 mph), a range of 1,930 km (1,200 miles) and a service ceiling of 7,620 m (25,000 ft). The B-25 was affectionately known as the 'Heavenly Body'.

➧ see B-29s Carry Out First Raid on Japan p. 168

The B–25 bomber.

MAY

The Battle of the Coral Sea took place in early May, the first major aircraft-carrier engagement of the war. In Europe, an assassination attempt was made on Reinhard Heydrich by two Czech agents, following which he died. The end of May saw the first thousand-bomber raid by the RAF on Cologne, inflicting terrible damage on the city.

4–8 May: Battle of the Coral Sea

This was the first major aircraft-carrier engagement of the war. In April 1942, Japanese forces left Rabaul to launch amphibious attacks on Port Moresby and Tulagi in the Solomon Islands. Three Japanese fleets set sail, but the US was alerted by intercepts.

Heavyweight Attacks

The Japanese successfully took Tulagi on 3 May, but the following day the USS *Yorktown* launched three air strikes, then sailed south to rendezvous with the *Lexington*. A second Japanese fleet headed for the Solomons and was attacked by B-17s on 6 May. The two fleets failed to find each other and on 8 May Japanese aircraft hit the two US carriers; *Lexington* was abandoned and scuttled, but the Japanese carrier *Shokaku* was also crippled. Meanwhile, the Allied surface fleet had come within range of the land-based Japanese aircraft on Rabaul and were attacked throughout the day. They were all that stood between the Japanese and Port Moresby. The Japanese panicked at the size of the US fleet and recalled their own. The *Yorktown* proceeded to Pearl Harbor, the *Shokaku* was out of action and the *Zuikaku* lacked aircraft.

The US aircraft carrier *Lexington* explodes.

5 May: Operation Ironclad

The British Force 121 landed unopposed near the main town of Diego Suarez on 5 May, in the first stage of the operation known as Ironclad. The Vichy French-held island of Madagascar initially resisted, but it was soon overcome. The Vichy retreated into the interior and continued to oppose the invasion and did not surrender until 6 November. Some 8,000 men were captured, along with vessels and aircraft.

see Pétain and Vichy France p. 42

27 May: Heydrich is Attacked in Prague

Two Czech agents working for the British were parachuted close to Prague in an assassination attempt on Reinhard Heydrich. They awaited him on a street corner, knowing his car would be forced to slow down. When the moment came, however, their machine guns jammed and instead they threw a grenade into the car. Despite being wounded, Heydrich returned fire with his pistol and then collapsed. He died on 4 June.

see Reinhard Heydrich p. 233

Thousand-Bomber Raid (30 May 1942)

The first RAF thousand-bomber raid (actually employing 1,047 bombers) struck Cologne on 30 May. They dropped 2,000 tons of bombs on the city, reducing 13,000 houses to rubble and damaging 6,000 more. The British lost around 40 bombers and 45 others were badly damaged. Of the raid Goering wrote 'Of course, the effects of aerial warfare are terrible if one looks at individual cases. But we have to accept them.' Even at this early stage it appears that Goering had accepted that Allied aircraft would be able to hit targets at will due to the impotence of his Luftwaffe.

Waves of bombers launch a raid over Germany.

JUNE

Following the Cologne raid, the RAF switched to blanket-bombing German industrial areas such as the Ruhr and Essen. The Battle of Midway took place between the Japanese and US fleets with a decisive US victory. In Czechoslovakia, German reprisals for Heydrich's murder in May were swift and brutal, resulting in thousands of arrests and deaths. At the end of June, Rommel successfully captured Tobruk and entered Egypt.

1941–45: Lancaster Bomber

The Lancaster, designed by Roy Chawick, made its maiden flight in January 1941. It was not an easy aircraft to construct as it consisted of 55,000 separate parts, it was therefore unsurprising that peak production only reached 293, in August 1944. Lancasters flew their first operational flight in March 1942; they accounted for 64 per cent of all of the bomb tonnage dropped by the RAF during the war and were immortalized as the aircraft that delivered the attacks during the Dambuster's raid and the sinking of the *Tirpitz*. Some 7,377 Lancasters were built, of which 3,932 were lost. In total, Lancasters flew 156,000 sorties and dropped 608,612 tons of bombs. Bomber Harris himself said of the Lancaster: 'The finest bomber of the war! Its efficiency was almost incredible, both in performance and in the way it could be saddled with ever-increasing loads without breaking the camel's back. The Lancaster won the naval war by destroying over one-third of the German submarines in their ports.... The Lancaster won the air war by taking the major part in forcing Germany to concentrate on building and using fighters to defend the Fatherland.'

› see USAAF Arrives in Britain p. 122

1 June: Royal Air Force Raids the Ruhr

Hard on the heels of the thousand-bomber raid on Cologne, the RAF switched targets to hit the Ruhr area and Essen – both major German industrial targets. This time the RAF mustered 1,036 bombers. Around 31 RAF aircraft were lost; this was an integral part of Bomber Harris's blanket bombing strategy, aimed at disrupting and ultimately destroying German morale and economy. The scale of the two attacks were four times larger than the worst raid London had so far suffered. At this point the RAF was using a mixture of bombers, including the Wellington, the Halifax, the Sterling and the Lancaster.

4–7 June: Battle of Midway

This engagement took place a month after the Battle of the Coral Sea and is considered by many to be the classic example of aircraft-carrier warfare. The Japanese hoped to destroy the US carrier fleet and thereby open up Hawaii to invasion. At dawn on 4 June, Japanese aircraft bombed Midway base. The US had broken the Japanese cipher codes, however, and Spruance, the commander of the US carrier group knew that if he hit the Japanese now they would be helpless as they attempted to refit and refuel their aircraft.

Survivors of the USS Yorktown.

Retaliatory Strikes

Spruance's attack, although costly, left three Japanese carriers ablaze. Japanese aircraft then crippled the USS *Yorktown*. A retaliatory strike from the USS *Enterprise* accounted for the final Japanese aircraft carrier, the *Hiryu*, along with the cruisers *Mogami* and *Mikuma*.

Decisive Victory

Spruance had won a decisive victory and promptly retired before Japanese submarines and surface vessels could find his carriers. The Japanese offensive ability had been destroyed; from this point Japan would be on the defensive. It had been just six months since the very same aircraft carriers had launched their aircraft against Pearl Harbor.

➧ see Pearl Harbor p. 97

1941–45: US Pacific Fleet v. Japanese Pacific Fleet

In assessing the relative strengths of the US and Japanese fleets on the eve of the US entry into the war, it is perhaps more useful to consider the combined Allied fleets despite the fact that they did not always operate under the same command. It should also be appreciated that at least half the available US vessels were actually engaged in the Atlantic and not the Pacific. Taking this into account it leaves the combined Allied fleet in the Pacific at 10 battleships, nine of which were American; one British battle cruiser; three American aircraft carriers; 14 heavy cruisers, one of which was American; 22 light cruisers, 11 of which were American, seven British, three Dutch and one French; 100 destroyers, of which 80 were American, 13 British and seven Dutch; and 69 submarines, 56 of which were American and 13 Dutch. The comparative balance in aircraft was considerably in the Japanese favour – the Allies could only muster 650 to the Japanese 1,540. Many of the Japanese ships were superior in design and in their weight-to-firepower ratios. In terms of the overall strength and effectiveness of the American Pacific fleet in particular, it was extremely providential that their aircraft carriers escaped the attack at Pearl Harbor.

➧ see Japanese High Watermark p. 124

10 June: Lidice Reprisals

German reprisals following the assassination of Heydrich were brutal. Three thousand Czechs were arrested; 2,000 were shot or died during interrogations. Czech police, under German orders, surrounded the village of Lidice (10 km/6 miles from Prague) rounding up the population. Killings began at 05:00 on 10 June; all men and boys were shot and the remaining civilians taken to concentration camps. Of the 300, 143 survived. The village was burned to the ground.

see Jews Deported from Warsaw p. 124

24 June: Rommel Captures Tobruk and Enters Egypt

By 12 June Rommel was within 24 km (15 miles) of Tobruk and British troops were retiring towards the Egyptian frontier. By 14 June Rommel's troops had reached the Tobruk perimeter. Within three days Tobruk was cut off and the bulk of the British army had retreated beyond Bardia by 19 June. On 21 June Klopper, the commander of Tobruk, requested authority to surrender and terms were discussed. Thirty-thousand men, 2,000 tons of petrol, 5,000 tons of food and 2,000 vehicles fell into Rommel's hands; 70 per cent of the Afrika Korps were dead.

see First Battle of El Alamein p. 128

Rommel's troops overcoming British traps in Tobruk.

JULY

Sevastopol in the Ukraine fell into German hands after heavy bombardment. The Germans now turned their attention to capturing the Caucasus oil fields. The USAAF, with its Flying Fortresses and Liberators, arrived in Britain; it carried out daylight bombing raids on Germany. Bomber Command intensified its attacks on Germany, causing widespread devastation of civilian and economic targets. The Japanese landed in New Guinea. Mid-July saw the evacuation of the Warsaw ghetto.

1 July: Germans Capture Sevastopol

Sevastopol had been cut off for months, its 100,000-strong garrison situated behind a triple defence line of trenches, minefields and forts. When the main barrage began on 2 June, all of the Luftwaffe 4's resources were thrown at the city, under the command of Wolfram von Richthofen. After suffering 46,000 shells and 20,000 tons of bombs, the defences began to crack and one by one the major forts were taken by German and Romanian troops. Finally, on 1 July, the defences were overrun and Sevastopol fell into German hands. The city had been besieged for 250 days. It was renamed Theodorichhafen by the Germans, and liberated by the Red Army in May 1944.

see Germans Drive for the Caucasus p. 123

1 July: USAAF Arrives in Britain

The lead elements of the 8th Army Air Force, flying B-17s, arrived in Prestwick in Britain on 1 July. The 8th would fly B-17 Flying Fortresses and B-24 Liberators in daylight bombing operations against Germany. Unlike Bomber Command, it was intended that they would make precision bombing runs; however, many of the results were indiscriminate and often equal damage was done to civilian targets.

1941–45: Flying Fortress

The first B-17 had its maiden flight on 28 July 1935, but by the time the US entered the war in December 1941 only a handful of the aircraft were in operation. The B-17 would be used primarily for daylight strategic bombing of enemy targets and by the time production ended in May 1945 some 12,726 of the aircraft had been built. The B-17 received its name the 'Flying Fortress' because of its awesome destructive fire power. In tight box formations it was perfectly capable of looking after itself with 13 machine guns bristling from its superstructure. B-17s flying out of Britain, mainly with the 8th Air Force, would endure an eight-hour return flight in order to bomb strategic targets in Germany. Until the last few months of the war many of these aircraft flew with no fighter escort. It has been estimated that around 4,735 of them were lost in combat missions during the war. It is believed that less than 15 are still capable of flight today, as most were scrapped in the post-war years, or sold as surplus. The jet aircraft was paramount in making the B-17 obsolete.

B–17 Flying Fortresses.

see Royal Air Force Raid Hamburg p. 125

9 July: Germans Drive for the Caucasus

In a change of strategy, the primary weight and thrust of the German assaults in Russia were diverted from the capture of Moscow to the overrunning of the Russian oil fields in the Caucasus. In the coming months this would have a massive impact on the outcome of the war. Army Group B was given the task of advancing on Stalingrad then along the River Volga towards Astrakhan.

see Germans Reach the Volga p. 128

11 July: Jews Deported from Warsaw

The Warsaw ghetto was created by the Germans in 1940 and served as a repository for Polish Jews before they were deported to one of the concentration or extermination camps – the first Jews departed the ghetto on 11 July. It has been estimated that 370,000 Jews from the Warsaw ghetto were killed. The deportation reached a climax in 1943, when it was no longer practicable to carry out executions in Warsaw on a mass scale.

1942–45: Zyklon B

Zyklon B was the commercial name given to the poison hydrogen cyanide. It was chosen by the Germans to produce quicker and more effective results in the extermination chambers housed in the concentration camps. The pellets or discs were originally developed as a powerful insecticide, but it was discovered that when they interacted with iron or concrete, they would release hydrogen cyanide gas. The gas entered the blood and produced a form of internal asphyxiation as it blocked the oxygen released from red blood cells. Zyklon B had been developed in Germany by I. G. Farben and it was used initially to control lice in the concentration camps.

➧ see Death Camps p. 125

21 July: Japanese High Watermark

Around 21 July 1942, the maximum expansion and conquest of the Japanese was reached when they landed on Gona and Buna in New Guinea. The US Solomon Islands Invasion Fleet was already on its way from New Zealand to rendezvous near Fiji. By 26 July the expeditionary force had rendezvoused with other units and was proceeding towards the Solomon Islands and by the end of the month US bombers were pounding Guadalcanal.

➧ see US Marines Land at Guadalcanal p. 126

Allied troops wait to catch Japanese snipers.

26–29 July: Royal Air Force Raid Hamburg

Harris and his Bomber Command, continuing the strategy of disrupting civilian and economic life in Germany, launched a series of raids, beginning on 26 July, on Hamburg, Danzig and other German targets. Harris promised to 'scourge the Third Reich from end to end'. In his broadcast in German, he told enemy civilians to expect air raids 'every night and every day, rain, blow or snow'.

see First USAAF Raid p. 127

1942–45: Death Camps

The term 'death camp' actually encompasses both the concentration camps and the extermination camps that collectively processed and held many millions of individuals during the war. The death camps were used to administer the German Final Solution and between 1941 and 1945 at least six million Jews alone were either slaughtered in or near their homes, by firing squads, murdered in mobile gas vans or in much larger numbers sent direct to extermination camps where they would be gassed. Many of the concentration camps, whilst ostensibly slave-labour facilities, simply meant a more lingering death from starvation and brutal treatment. The major concentration camps were Dachau, Sachsenhausen, Buchenwald, Mauthausen, Flossenburg, Ravensbruck, Auschwitz, Natzweiler, Neuengamme and Gross-rosen.

see Extermination Camps Become Operational p. 64

AUGUST

The planned liberation of the Solomon Islands from the Japanese began this month, with a large US force landing on Guadalcanal. Stalin and Churchill met at the first Moscow conference to discuss war aims. The USAAF made its first raid on Europe this month, and Mountbatten launched a disastrous Allied raid on Dieppe. In the Western Desert, the battle of Alam el Halfa took place with Rommel's side failing to gain the initiative.

7 August: US Marines Land at Guadalcanal

Early on 7 August, US marines began landing on Guadalcanal as part of the operations associated with the liberation of the Solomon Islands. Over the next few days waves of Japanese aircraft attacked fleets supporting the marines. By 8 August the marines had built an airstrip on Guadalcanal and by 19 August there were 11,000 US troops on the island. Throughout August and September the Japanese continued to reinforce and there was vicious fighting throughout September and October; neither side made headway. After further battles on land and sea, the US finally gained control of the island by February. Japanese losses were estimated at 9,000; US losses were in excess of 2,000.

see Battle of the Bismarck Sea p. 137

Battle for Guadalcanal.

12 August: Stalin and Churchill Meet in Moscow

This was the first Moscow conference, attended by Stalin, Churchill and Averell Harriman (representing Roosevelt), as well as a representative for de Gaulle. The meeting continued until 15 August and discussed the possibility of opening a second front in Europe. Stalin demanded that pressure be taken off his armies; Churchill, not yet prepared, felt a demonstration would come in the form of the Dieppe raid.

➧ see Casablanca Conference p. 134

17 August: First USAAF Raid

Escorted by RAF Spitfires, 12 B-17 Flying Fortresses of the 8th US Army Air Force – which had arrived in Britain the previous month – launched their first major bombing attack on German-held Europe. The targets were the railway yards at Rouen in France. Between August 1942 and the end of the year, B-17s and B-24s (which began arriving in September) would make 1,547 flights, losing 32 aircraft.

1939–45: Liberator

Although some 19,256 B-24 Liberators were constructed, it is still a lesser-known aircraft than the B-17 Flying Fortress. After making its maiden flight in December 1939, the aircraft was deployed primarily in daytime bombing raids, initially without fighter support. Collectively, Liberators dropped 630,000 tons of bombs during the war, operating in all the major theatres of conflict. In addition to their bombing duties, others flew mine-laying missions, carried cargo and fuel and went on photographic reconnaissance missions. The Liberator was variously known as Ford's Folly or the Flying Box Car.

➧ see USAAF Targets Germany p. 135

19 August: Dieppe Raid

Under the direction of Lord Mountbatten, a major Allied raid was launched on Dieppe on 19 August. The force arrived off the coast at 03:00. Things began to go seriously wrong when

troops landed on the wrong beach and the invasion fleet ran into enemy vessels. The Canadians landed on the main beach and were pinned down instantly; their Churchill tanks were trapped. By 09:00 it was apparent that the raid had been a failure. Fifteen hundred prisoners were taken by the Germans, 28 tanks were lost, as well as several vessels and, in the skies above, the Allies lost 95 aircraft but shot down over 80 German aircraft and damaged a further 100 planes.

› see Louis Mountbatten p. 238

1942–45: Churchill Tank

The Churchill was designed to replace the Matilda. In March 1942 a major redesign led to the Mk III. Churchill Mks I and II were used in Dieppe in August 1942, with deep-wading equipment. The Churchill proved its worth, particularly during the Italian campaign. The Mk VI began production in November 1943. Churchills were converted for a variety of specialized roles, notably the Assault Vehicle Royal Engineers (AVRE), which was designed for carpet-laying (that is, enabling passage over soft ground), bridge-laying and mine-clearing.

› see D-Day Beaches p. 164

28 August: Germans Reach the Volga

In their push towards Stalingrad, advanced units of the German army reached the River Volga on 28 August, and had pushed forward to the western suburbs of the city by 3 September. The battle for Stalingrad began its first phase with massive German air assaults supporting the ground troops. Both sides poured in reinforcements and reserves, the weather deteriorated and by 13 September, after four weeks, the German 6th Army controlled the bulk of the city.

› see Battle of Stalingrad p. 130

30 August: First Battle of El Alamein

On 30 August Rommel launched an offensive along the whole of the El Alamein front. The battle became known as Alam el Halfa as it was mainly concentrated around this ridge, to

Forces landing before the Battle of El Alamein.

the south-east of El Alamein. Rommel intended to turn the British positions and surround the 8th Army. By the following day it was clear that he was failing. The RAF, the 7th Armoured Division, minefields and a shortage of fuel all proved insurmountable obstacles. On 1 September he tried again but was driven back, by which time the British had the initiative and were preparing to counterattack. By 2 September Rommel's troops had fallen back to their starting line to wait for a British counteroffensive that never materialized.

Desert Rats (1939–45)

The British 8th Army comprised a mixture of British and Commonwealth forces. Collectively they were dubbed the 'Desert Rats', as their war was waged surrounded by sand. By November 1941, when Operation Crusader was launched, the 8th Army was effectively two British Corps, the XIII and XXX. As the campaign in North Africa developed, the 8th Army acquired X Corps, plus several other smaller armoured units.

➧ see Second Battle of El Alamein p. 131

SEPTEMBER–NOVEMBER

The beginning of the battle for Stalingrad between the Russians and Germans took place in September, with fierce fighting on both sides for this key city. A major turning point came following the Allied victory in the Second Battle of El Alamein, ending Axis hopes of occupying Egypt, taking control of the Suez Canal and gaining access to the Middle Eastern oil fields. Operation Torch, in early November, saw the British-American invasion of northwest Africa, another Allied victory.

15 September–2 February 1943: Battle of Stalingrad

The Russian defence of Stalingrad was both determined and ferocious, despite massive air attacks and ground assaults; they stubbornly held and contested every inch, resulting in bitter house-to-house fighting. By the beginning of October German impetus had petered out and by 11 October, after 51 days of fighting, they had made little forward movement. On 14 October Russian reserves were moved into position and four days later the Germans renewed their assault.

Building debris on the outskirts of the besieged city of Stalingrad.

Russian Victory

On 18 November the Russians launched a huge offensive; they threatened to cut the Germans off in Stalingrad by attacking the weaker flanks. Within four days 250,000 Germans had been trapped. The German commander Paulus made desperate attempts to break out and outside attempts to break in failed. By 31 January Paulus was forced to surrender.

see Siege of Leningrad p. 88

23 October–5 November: Second Battle of El Alamein

The second Battle of El Alamein was in fact two operations masterminded by General Montgomery. The first, Operation Lightfoot, opened on 23 October; it saw the greatest concentration of Allied artillery so far in the war. Montgomery had an advantage of 2:1 in men, tanks and aircraft. Characteristically, however, the Germans reacted swiftly and Montgomery's first operation was thwarted by Rommel's counterattacks.

Operation Supercharge

Montgomery launched a second major offensive, Operation Supercharge, on 2 November. This time his armour managed to penetrate the minefields and by the evening Rommel had just 32 tanks left in action. Rommel now faced disaster: his Italian support troops were being wiped out and despite Hitler's instructions not to retreat, he ordered a withdrawal on 4 November. The British advance continued, Tobruk fell on 13 November followed by Benghazi on 20 November.

➧ see Bernard Montgomery p. 237

8–11 November: Operation Torch

Operation Torch, the planned invasion of Vichy-held north-west Africa by Allied troops, witnessed a vast amphibious landing that significantly involved US troops. Although Torch would be overshadowed by Operation Overlord in 1944, it was nonetheless an overwhelming show of force. Landings began on 8 November and, in a politically sensitive situation, Frenchmen were forced to fight their compatriots. Vichy troops initially showed determined opposition. Pétain received a letter from Roosevelt, imploring him to throw his support behind the Anglo-American invasion. Pétain passed the decision to his High Commissioner in Algiers, but outwardly assured the Germans of his support. However, by 11 November it had become clear to the Vichy authorities that continued resistance would be useless and at 07:00 the ceasefire came into force. Germany realized that the Vichy French had no stomach to fight the Allies, so on the same day German troops marched into unoccupied France.

➧ see British Enter Libya and Tunisia p. 135

1943

JANUARY AND FEBRUARY

In January the Allied leaders met at Casablanca to discuss new strategy. Meanwhile, the Allied air fleets were set to concentrate on destroying German industry, and ground was gained in North Africa.

14–24 January: Casablanca Conference

Although only Roosevelt and Churchill amongst the big three leaders were able to attend the Casablanca Conference, the Russians were represented by key officials. Stalin was adamant that the Anglo-Americans should open a second front in Europe, arguing that Germany would surely crumble if it faced a war on two fronts. While Roosevelt supported a French landing, Churchill preferred Italy, describing it as the 'soft underbelly of Europe'. This would enable the Allies to link up with Russian troops in the Balkans. In return for agreeing to an invasion of France in 1944, Roosevelt committed to landings in Sicily and Italy.

see Roosevelt, Churchill and Stalin Meet at Teheran p. 149

General Giraud, Roosevelt, de Gaulle and Churchill at the Casablanca Conference.

1940–45: Sturmovik

The Sturmovik, deployed by the Russians in World War II, was generally used as a ground-support aircraft. They were effective in their role, but casualties of the aircraft and pilots were extremely high. The improved version first appeared on the battlefield in October 1942. The aircraft was heavily armoured in comparison with the German aircraft it would face and it became the most feared Russian aircraft on the Eastern Front. It was cheap and straightforward to manufacture and consequently over 36,000 were built. Its cannons were capable of penetrating virtually any German tank. Vast numbers roamed the battlefields, making daytime movement extremely hazardous.

23 January: British Enter Libya and Tunisia

In the three months after the El Alamein offensive by Montgomery's 8th Army, Allied troops entered the last Italian-held city of Mussolini's North African empire. The 11th Hussars arrived in Tripoli at dawn on 23 January and by noon the Union Jack had been set flying over the central square. Ten days previously, General Leclerc's Free French had joined Montgomery's men and driven across the Tunisian border in pursuit of Rommel's Afrika Korps.

see Kasserine Pass p. 137

27 January: USAAF Targets Germany

The attack on the German warehousing and industrial plant at Wilhelmshaven by the US 8th Air Force was the air raid that set the pattern for operations over the next 18 months. Over 60 B-17 Flying Fortresses and B-24s hit Wilhemshaven, while others attacked Copenhagen and Dusseldorf. To coincide with broadcasts by Goering and Goebbels – who stated German victory as assured – the RAF made daylight attacks on Berlin and saturation attacks on Hamburg.

see The Dambusters p. 139

US Flying Fortresses.

1943–45: The Chindits and Merrill's Marauders

The Chindits, named after the mythical 'Chinthe' beasts that guard Burmese temples, was a multi-national force of 3,000 men led by Orde C. Wingate. Wingate's tactics were revolutionary: he split troops into mixed columns of 300, each led by a major, which contained a cross-section of all arms. These columns terrorized the Japanese in Burma and specialized in hit-and-run missions. With the support of No. 7 Air Commando, the seemingly impossible had been achieved. At the height of the operations they were supplying and supporting 14 British, five Gurkha, three West African and two Burmese battalions, some 20,000 troops.

Wingate's guerillas.

Inspired by the Chindits, in August 1943, volunteers formed a US long-range penetration unit, codenamed *Galahad*. In January 1944 the unit was placed under the command of Brigadier General Frank Merrill. They fought 35 battles against the Japanese, with one particularly hard-won action in March 1944. Their objectives were Shaduzup and Inkangahtawng but the group were forced to withdraw, pursued by Japanese. By 31 March the American garrison was isolated at Nhpum Ga and subjected to increasingly ferocious attacks by the Japanese. The Marauders put up an impressive fight and eventually, on 9 April, the Japanese withdrew, having lost 400 men – but not before the unit had lost over 50 men, with many more injured and sick.

FEBRUARY AND MARCH

In February the Germans were beaten back in the Atlas Mountains, but many Allied lives were lost. March brought success in the Bismarck Sea and disappointment in a failed plot against Hitler.

14–25 February: Kasserine Pass

Initially German troops made headway in their attempt on 14 February to break through the Allied defences around the Kasserine Pass in the Atlas Mountains, but Montgomery's 8th Army was pushing up on the Mareth Line and by 22 February, with British troops arriving to support the Americans, Rommel began to break off the attacks. Two days later Allied troops re-entered Kasserine. Allied casualties reached 10,000, over half of which were American, against a loss of 2,000 to the Axis powers.

see Fall of Tunis p. 139

3–5 March: Battle of the Bismarck Sea

Eight Japanese transport ships, escorted by eight destroyers en route to New Guinea, were intercepted by US aircraft. The Japanese lacked air cover, as American and Australian aircraft had pounded Japanese airfields. All the Japanese transports were sunk as well as four of the destroyers in an important tactical victory for General MacArthur.

see Operation Vengeance p. 138

13 March: Failed Assassination Attempt on Hitler

Henning von Tresckow was a senior German army officer who had fought on the Eastern Front between 1941 and the middle of 1943. He led a conspiracy to assassinate Hitler – an elaborate attempt that involved placing a bomb on Hitler's aircraft when it left Smolensk on 13 March. The attempt failed but von Tresckow remained undetected and after the July plot failure, committed suicide.

APRIL AND MAY

April and May saw several morale-boosting actions and displays of power from the Allies, with the elimination of Yamamoto, the fall of Tunis and the Dambusters raid. However, meanwhile, unthinkable killing was happening in Warsaw.

18 April: Operation Vengeance

Having intercepted Japanese ciphers and radio messages, US forces became aware that Admiral Yamamoto would be en route to Bougainville on 18 April. Yamamoto was the architect of the Pearl Harbor attack and Operation Vengeance was set in motion when US P-38s of the 13th Air Force left Guadalcanal and shot down Yamamoto's aircraft over Bougainville. It was a crippling strategic and moral loss for the Japanese, and a considerable morale booster for America.

➧ see Isokoru Yamamoto p. 245

19 April–16 May: Warsaw Ghetto

The Warsaw ghetto was a vast city prison containing 400,000 Jews. In four weeks from 19 April 1943, SS troops and Gestapo units under the command of SS Brigadier-General Stroop, slaughtered over 56,000 men, women and children in the ghetto. Stroop would later claim that he had been working under orders from Hitler to eliminate the ghetto and its inhabitants. Although the ghetto dwellers had tried to resist, the surrounding 3-m (10-ft) wall had trapped them. The SS, Gestapo and Ukrainian troops were aided in the massacre by Jewish collaborators and policemen. Stroop himself was sentenced to death at an American court hearing in Dachau in March 1947. Sentence was carried out by hanging at the scene of his crimes, Warsaw, in September 1951.

➧ see Oradour-Sur-Glane Massacre p. 168

6–13 May: Fall of Tunis

At dawn on 6 May the British 1st Army began its long-planned assault on Tunis. The British forces were supported to the south by French troops and to the north by US forces heading for Bizerta. Von Arnim had recently replaced Rommel as commander but he was powerless to stop the onslaught. At 15:40 on 7 May British troops entered Tunis, narrowly beating the US entry into Bizerta at 16:15. What remained of the Axis forces withdrew to the Cape Bon peninsular. Officially fighting ended at 11:00 on 9 May in north-east Tunisia, but the fighting continued over the following two days until finally Von Arnim surrendered to Montgomery, leading his 250,000 German and Italian troops into captivity. The war in North Africa was over.

see Operation Husky p. 141

12–25 May: Trident Conference in Washington

The Trident Conference approved the plans for Operation Husky – the landings in Sicily that were scheduled for 10 July. A date was also set for Operation Overlord (the D-Day landings), with a provisional date of May 1944. The first target, however, would be Italy, with the aim of knocking the country out of the war. The outline strategy in the Pacific was also approved.

see Operation Overlord p. 161

16 May: The Dambusters

No. 617 Squadron was formed at Scampton in March to launch Operation Chastise, the bombing and breeching of three vital dams in the Ruhr region. The mission was led by Guy Gibson, who was given permission to poach any Lancaster crew he felt suitable for the job. The attack required low-level precision bombing over water and for weeks not even Gibson was told what the target would be.

see Guy Gibson p. 230

Dambuster leader Guy Gibson.

The Target

The bomb, designed by Barnes Wallace, was a mine that had to be dropped at exactly 18 m (60 ft), at a speed of 354 kph (220 mph). Nineteen Lancasters were modified to carry out the attack, which was scheduled for 16–17 May. The targets were the Mohne, the Eder and the Sorpe dams. These provided 75 per cent of the electrical power for German industry in the Ruhr basin.

A 'bouncing bomb'.

Success?

The Mohne and the Eder dams were successfully destroyed, but eight aircraft were lost during the raid. The Germans managed to repair the dams quickly and the Ruhr area was soon back in production. The raid was one of the most audacious operations of the war, proving that no German target was too difficult to deter the Allies from attempting its destruction.

JULY

In July action continued in all corners: the Russians gained the upper hand in the east for the rest of the war, the Allies gained a foothold in Sicily, tensions escalated in the South Pacific, and Hamburg received severe bombing from the British and the Americans.

5–16 July: Operation Citadel

The Germans launched their last major offensive in the east, Operation Citadel (the Battle of Kursk) on 5 July. The engagement took place on a 322-km (200-mile) front. The Germans had massed 2,000 tanks, including their new Panthers and Tigers and were covered by 2,000 aircraft. The Russians were heavily dug in with up to seven defensive lines. There was ferocious combat; collectively the engagement involved 6,000 tanks, 4,000 aircraft and two million men. With the numbers of dead and wounded mounting, the German assaults began to peter out and on 12 July the Russians went on the offensive. The Germans withdrew; Operation Citadel had failed.

10 July: Operation Husky

The long-awaited invasion of Europe – codenamed Operation Husky – began with Allied landings in Sicily on 10 July. One hundred and sixty thousand men and 600 tanks were deployed against an estimated 300,000 Italians and 90,000 Germans. The landings were preceded by raids from Special Forces. The following day Italian and German units launched a counterattack. Although the Italians were beaten off easily, the Germans proved tougher opposition and their tanks managed to penetrate to within a mile of the landing beaches. Meanwhile, British troops, having landed at Syracuse, drove up the coast to Augusta.

1941–45: The Tigers

Before May 1941, the Germans considered their lighter tanks adequate in battlefield actions, but after encountering heavier vehicles, they produced the Tiger I, the most powerful tank of its time. Tiger II, first encountered by Russian troops in May 1944, resembled a larger, up-gunned Panther and had a new and simpler designed turret. In the autumn of 1944, German tank production was rationalized and the Tiger II and the Panther remained the only two turreted tanks to be kept in production for 1945.

➧ see Russian Winter Offensive p. 149

The 'Tiger' tank.

Turning the Tide

By 12 July, two days after the operation was launched, the majority of German and Italian forces were withdrawing northwards. The foothold on Sicily had been achieved; the Americans alone had taken 18,000 prisoners. The race for Messina was now on.

➧ see Race for Messina p. 144

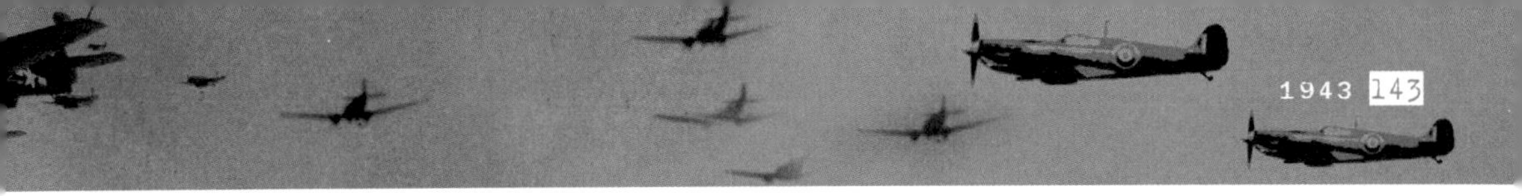

17 July 1943–24 March 1944: Bougainville

The battle for Bougainville began with a naval engagement between the US and Japanese fleets on 17 July and the fighting would fluctuate in intensity for many months. The last large-scale action took place on 24 March 1944, when a massive American counterattack succeeding in halting the Japanese, although skirmishing would continue as late as May.

24–25 July: Mussolini is Censured and Imprisoned

The meeting of the Fascist Grand Council took place while Allied troops were wrestling control of Sicily on 24 July. Italy had already lost North Africa and hundreds of thousands of men. It was now time for a regime change and Mussolini lost the vote of confidence. The following day the Italian leader was arrested and imprisoned. He was replaced by Badoglio, who determined that Italy would continue the war. The Germans immediately sent eight divisions south.

➧ see Skorzeny Snatches Mussolini p. 147

24 July–3 August: Hamburg Raids

On 24 July the RAF made a massive night raid on Hamburg. At 08:00 the following morning Berlin radio reported 'all Hamburg seems to be in flames'. Indeed it was – 20,000 people had been killed and 60,000 seriously injured. The RAF had employed some 740 bombers and had used tinfoil strips to confuse the German radar systems. The US would add their weight on 25–26 July. Waves of bombers continued to pound the city; it was estimated that at least 40,000 civilian deaths were caused by the time the raids ended on 3 August. The worst of the assault came on the night of 27 July, when a wind-whipped, three-hour-long firestorm was created. Even the roads were alight as the asphalt melted in the heat of the fires. This was the heaviest raid suffered so far by Germany.

➧ see Operation Tidalwave p. 144

AUGUST

August was mainly characterised by an Allied determination to take out German military and industrial capacity by concentrated bombing raids, while the race to Messina was won by the US.

1 August: Operation Tidal Wave

In line with the agreements made at the Trident Conference, Operation Tidal Wave was launched on 1 August. One hundred and seventy-seven B-24 Liberators of the US 9th Air Force hit Romanian oil fields, knocking out 40 per cent of their production capacity. The costs were high and 54 of the aircraft together with 232 air crew were lost. The Ploesti oil refineries would continue to be a target for the Allies.

12–17 August: Race for Messina

With German and Italian forces in retreat, the British and Americans stepped up the pressure to be the first to reach Messina, at the north-eastern tip of Sicily. Ultimately, the US 3rd Division would claim the prize at 10:15 on 17 August. The capture of the whole island had taken 39 days, but the majority of the Germans – some 60,000 – had escaped to the mainland with their equipment.

see George Patton p. 239

17 August: Operation Double Strike

Operation Double Strike saw the first major US daylight raid over Germany. Their targets were aircraft and ball-bearings factories. The losses were high, however, and around 36 aircraft failed to return to their bases. A larger raid was planned for 14 October, a day that became known as Black Thursday for its even greater losses.

A German V2 rocket being launched at Peenemünde.

RAF Bombs Peenemünde

During the night of 17–18 August, nearly 600 RAF bombers struck the V1 and V2 factories at Peenemünde, the central production centre for the Doodlebugs and the new V2 rocket being developed by Werner von Braun. Some 1,500 tons of explosives and incendiaries were dropped hoping to stop, or at the very least cripple, the continued construction and development of German rocket technology. The Peenemünde raid, occurring on the same day as the fall of Messina, proved a temporary respite for German cities, but a renewed Anglo-American bomber offensive would soon rain thousands more tons of bombs on German industry and civilian targets.

see Werner von Braun p. 227

17–24 August: Roosevelt and Churchill Meet in Quebec

Roosevelt and Churchill confirmed their agreement of the launching of Operation Overlord for May 1944, but for the time being they agreed to give priority to Operation Pointblank, whose aim was to cripple German industry. They also approved the invasion of the Italian mainland and drew out the strategies that would be employed in the Pacific against the Japanese. Mountbatten was placed in command of the South-East Asia front.

see Operation Overlord p. 161

SEPTEMBER

September finally brought the capitulation of Italy, turning the tide more fiercely against the Germans, who despite this and the Allied landings in Salerno, managed to seize Rome and rescue their remaining Italian friend, Mussolini. After their surrender the Italians on Cephalonia were doomed to German reprisals.

3 September: Allies Land in Southern Italy

At 04:30 on 3 September, Montgomery's 8th Army landed on mainland Italy. This was essentially a diversionary attack, as the main landings would take place at Salerno, but they met with little resistance. At 17:50 the same day, on the island of Sicily, Castellano signed an armistice on behalf of Badoglio. Italy would be out of the war in less than a week.

US troops landing on the beach in Italy.

8–10 September: Italy Surrenders; Allies and Germany Move In

Developments in Italy were occurring at a rapid pace. The 8th Army was driving inland and on 8 September Operation Avalanche, the main Allied landings in Italy, took place at Salerno. The troops began wading ashore at 17:30, coinciding with an announcement by Eisenhower that the Italians had made an unconditional surrender. At 21:45 Badoglio confirmed the statement, as Germans concentrated their troops to deal with the Salerno landings.

Operation Slapstick and Germans Seize Rome

The full landings took place at 03:30 on 9 September and British paratroops launched Operation Slapstick, capturing Taranto. Already there was widespread fighting between Italian troops and the Germans, who were by now moving in on Rome. The Italian royal family had fled to Brindisi. German troops seized Rome on 10 September after skirmishes with Italian troops. Elsewhere, Montgomery was holding a line from Catanzaro to Nicastro and on 11 September the British 1st Airborne Division took Brindisi. The German position was becoming increasingly precarious.

12 September: Skorzeny Snatches Mussolini

SS Lieutenant Colonel Otto Skorzeny was the man charged with rescuing Mussolini from imprisonment. When Il Duce's location at Gran Sasso in Abruzzo was finally discovered, Skorzeny's commandos, using the element of surprise, landed in a glider, charged into the rooms and fled with the Italians before a shot could be fired. Mussolini was taken to Rome in a light aircraft, where he boarded another aircraft bound for Vienna.

➧ see Benito Mussolini p. 238

Italian leader Benito Mussolini.

13–26 September: Cephalonia Massacre

On 8 September, the new Italian government announced the cessation of hostilities against the Allies. For the 12,000-strong Italian garrison on the Greek island of Cephalonia, this presented problems. The Italians, commanded by Russian Front veteran, Antonio Gaudin, fought pitched battles against German forces under Major von Hirschfeld, supported by Stuka dive bombers. After the Italian surrender to them, the Germans shot 4,750 of the men; a further 3,000 died when the transport ships heading for Germany hit mines. In all over 10,000 Italians were killed.

OCTOBER–DECEMBER

Italy was now suffering after its defection, and the US was suffering huge losses in the continued effort to smash German industry. However, Russia stormed forward, pushing out the Germans and liberating their towns and cities; and Allied strikes were made against Japanese targets.

THE STAR
SURRENDER OF ITALY
ITALIANS 'DEMOB' ARMY?
All The Armed Forces: Armistice Now In Force
ITALIANS ASKED TO HELP TO EJECT GERMANS

The Evening News
LATE EXTRA
ITALY SURRENDERS
Unconditional Capitulation Of All Her Armed Forces: Armistice Granted
STALINO IS CAPTURED

Evening Standard
ITALY: UNCONDITIONAL SURRENDER—OFFICIAL
Eisenhower Announces the News by Radio
She Has Been Granted An Armistice
NOON RAID ON SUBURBS OF ROME
HITLER HAS NEW ARMS DICTATOR
GERMANS EVACUATE STALINO
ALEXANDER IN ITALY

Italy surrenders to the Allies.

13 October: Italy Declares War on Germany

On 13 October Badoglio declared war on Germany. He urged Italian soldiers to resist the Germans to the last man; Badoglio had little option, with overwhelming Allied forces already in Italy and the Germans carrying out widespread looting. All across the country Germans were taking reprisals against Italians and there were random shootings and destruction of buildings.

➧ see Monte Cassino p. 153

14 October: Black Thursday

US aircraft of the 8th Air Force launched another attack on the ball-bearing factories. Some 300 aircraft were involved in the raid, which occurred unescorted in daylight. US Air Force casualties were enormous, and this raid, known as Black Thursday because of the severity of the losses, achieved little and the ball-bearing factories were hardly touched. Daylight raids continued in ever-increasing intensity and on 3 November, 500 US 8th Air Force bombers devastated Wilhelmshafen Harbour.

➧ see USAAF Seizes Command of the Air p. 152

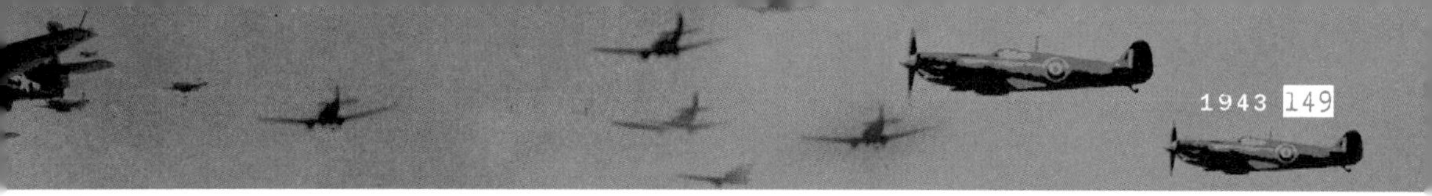

6 November: Kiev Liberated

On 4 November Russian troops had created a bridgehead on the River Dniepr and threatened to surround Kiev. By the following day German troops were in danger of being surrounded. On 6 November they withdrew, leaving behind them the wreckage of Kiev's most beautiful buildings, but the third largest city in Russia was back in friendly hands.

28–30 November: Roosevelt, Churchill and Stalin Meet at Teheran

Stalin, Roosevelt and Churchill met for a conference codenamed Eureka. Priority was given to Operation Overlord and Anvil, which would be an Allied landing in southern France. Stalin undertook to join in the war against Japan as soon as the Germans were beaten. It was proposed that January 1944 be the date for the invasion of the Marshall Islands and New Britain. New Guinea was recaptured by June and the Mariana Islands liberated by October 1944.

» see Marshall Islands p. 155

15 December: Operation Dexterity

Codenamed Operation Dexterity, this was the Australian-American amphibious landing in New Britain. It was completed on 15 December and Japanese resistance swiftly overcome. By 24 December US bombers were ranging far and wide, hitting Japanese targets across all of New Britain.

24 December: Russian Winter Offensive

Although the Russians had launched an offensive on the Ukrainian front on 10 December, the major blow took place in the Kiev area. The Germans resisted, but the Russians quickly took key positions and began pressing forward. By 26 December over 150 Russian towns and villages had been liberated. By 31 December Vitebsk was virtually surrounded and by 2 January 1944 they were just 29 km (18 miles) from the original Polish border. They encountered stiff German opposition, but on 7 January the Russians broke through again, trapping large numbers of German troops behind them.

» see Battle of the Dniepr p. 156

1944

JANUARY

While the US now had the run of the skies, things were not going so smoothly on land, with the drawn out battle for Italy against the Germans and the bloody and ferocious fight for control of the Marshall Islands, which were in the way of the path to Japan.

11 January: USAAF Seizes Control of the Air

In January, the US Air Force received a vital addition to its armoury in the form of the P-51 Mustang. This fighter aircraft and interceptor had the capacity to accompany US bombers all the way to their targets and back. This now meant that German aircraft could not interdict Allied daylight raids without running the risk of suffering huge casualties from these fast and highly manoeuvrable aircraft.

The American plane 'Thunderbolt'.

1939–45: Lightning and Thunderbolt

The P-38 Lightning was probably the most advanced aircraft of its time when it first flew on 27 January 1939. It was developed under strict secrecy, and its strength was its design, speed (666 kph/414 mph) and range (3,636 km/2,259 miles). The Lightning was a great all-round performer; it could out-run and out-distance the opposition. When it came into operation in 1942 it could beat anything put in the air by the Axis Powers. The P-47 Thunderbolt was the most famous US aircraft of the war, with over 15,600 built. It was originally conceived as an interceptor, but it was also used as a heavy fighter, high-altitude escort and a fighter bomber. It made its first combat flight over Europe in April 1943. The Thunderbolt was a sturdy and rugged aircraft that would serve in all theatres for several Allied air forces.

1942–53: Mustang

The Mustang (P-51) was originally designed at Britain's request and called the NA-73. The USAAF purchased some early versions for use as ground-support aircraft. It was modified to give it a greater speed (703 kph/437 mph) and a higher ceiling altitude; the initial prototypes were built in 1942, but by 1943 they had entered service and combat over Europe. The Mustang became the ultimate high-altitude escort for the USAAF B-17 and B-24 bombers. Its role as interceptor proved unbeatable and the aircraft accounted for nearly 5,000 German aircraft kills during the war. Mustangs also saw combat in other theatres, including the Pacific. In all, some 14,855 Mustangs were built during the war for the USAAF, staying in service until 1953.

12 January–17 May: Monte Cassino

Monte Cassino, 161 km (100 miles) south-east of Rome, was the pivotal point on the German-held Gustav Line. The Allies had bombed the town of Cassino as early as 10 September 1943, but by the time the Allies reached the area the Germans had dug in. The first Allied assault took place on 17 January, to coincide with the Anzio landings. It was a

disaster and a second assault was planned for 15 February. The attack was preceded by an intense bombardment. New Zealand infantry seized the town, whilst US troops secured Snakeshead Hill. The third attack took place on 15 March, with Gurkhas, New Zealanders and Poles all involved in the assault. Cassino would not fall until 17 May.

A New Zealand soldier aiming his rifle during the attack on Monte Cassino.

16 January: Eisenhower Becomes Commander

On 16 January General Dwight Eisenhower was appointed Supreme Commander of Allied invasion forces in Europe or more precisely, Head of Supreme Headquarters Allied Expeditionary Force (SHAEF). He would therefore be in place to oversee all European operations, including the proposed Operation Overlord and Anvil.

➤ see Dwight D. Eisenhower p. 230

22 January–4 June: Anzio and the Fall of Rome

Within 24 hours of the landings, codenamed Operation Shingle, 36,000 Allied troops reached within 48 km (30 miles) of Rome. They met little opposition and it seemed that the road to Rome was clear. Rather than causing the Germans severe difficulties and forcing them to abandon Rome, the vast army simply sat and waited for the Germans to come to them. As a result, Rome remained in German hands until 4 June, when elements of General Mark Clark's 9th Army entered the city. In truth, the Anzio landings, although they had been a singular failure, had drawn the bulk of the German troops to them, where they had been comprehensively defeated. Their demise would hasten the fall of Italy.

see Operation Dragoon-Anvil p. 179

An American Sherman tank going ashore at Anzio in Italy.

30 January: Marshall Islands

Forty-thousand men were earmarked to deal with the 8,000 Japanese defenders of the Marshall Islands. The primary problem was that the 2,000 islands and islets extended some 998 km (620 miles) and had to be taken in order to push towards Japan. The Japanese had dug in on nearly all the major positions, and despite the fact that US aircraft had been pounding the islands and Japanese shipping for a considerable time, they were still to put up a fanatical defence. Based on previous experience, the islands were saturated with explosives before the marines landed. Even then many of the defenders had escaped certain death. Throughout the whole campaign every inch of every island would be contested in the most ferocious manner. Casualties would be high for both belligerents.

see New Guinea p. 159

FEBRUARY

As the battle for Kwajalein ended, operations continued to proceed on other islands in the southern sectors and Tojo became dictator of a Japan that was losing ground. Meanwhile, some 75,000 Germans perished in the action at Dniepr.

4 February: Nimitz Becomes Governor of the Marshall Islands

In recognition that the struggle for the Marshall Islands would continue for some time, Chester Nimitz was placed in command of the operations. On the same day Japanese resistance on Kwajalein ceased, having cost the US 177 dead and 1,000 wounded. Some 4,800 Japanese had been killed or were missing and just 41 had been taken prisoner.

➧ see Chester Nimitz p. 239

6–9 February: Battle of the Dniepr

On 6 February the Russians captured Apostolovo, a vital railroad junction, and trapped five divisions of the German 6th Army. Over the next two days the Russians systematically annihilated the German bridgehead over the River Dniepr. Continued pressure on the rest of the front ensured the liberation of the Ukraine and the recapture of the Crimea by May 1944. On 17 February the Korsun-Shevchenkovsky pocket was finally eliminated by the Russians.

➧ see Sevastopol is Liberated p. 160

21 February: Tojo Becomes Dictator

General Hideki Tojo, the Japanese Prime Minister, assumed the position of the Chief of the Japanese Army General Staff, replacing Field Marshall Sugiyama, effectively making him the military dictator of Japan. Tojo took over at a time when Japanese forces were being forced back on all fronts.

➧ see Hideki Tojo p. 244

MARCH–MAY

March and April were characterised by action against the defiant Japanese, in Burma, India, China and New Guinea. There was also success with the British Royal Navy's attack on the German warship Tirpitz. In May Russia gained valuable ground over the Germans.

March: Behind Enemy Lines

An integral part of the operations against the Japanese in Burma was the insertion of troops deep behind enemy lines. Amongst the most famous of the units involved were Merrill's Marauders and the Chindits. One of the most stunning operations occurred from March 1944, when Chindit units, directed by Mountbatten, established an air strip behind Japanese lines in Burma, precipitating a series of running battles in the jungle against the Japanese.

see Joseph Stilwell p. 243, The Chindits and Merrill's Marauders p. 136

Wingate's guerillas behind Japanese lines.

April–July: Ichi-Go Offensive

The Japanese launched a two-pronged offensive from April. The first was aimed at Burma, but the Chinese part of the campaign made great strides against the Chinese Nationalists led by Chiang Kai-shek and destroyed many of their best divisions. The Nationalists were poorly led and inefficient, even after seven years of war. The Japanese managed to clear Henan Province and it is certain that this offensive improved the long-term interests of Mao Tse-tung.

see Mao Tse-tung p. 236

DAILY EXPRESS

Barracuda reports reveal truth about Hitler's only battleship

BOMBS MAKE TIRPITZ 'SELESS AS A WARSHIP'

Here it is—the first picture of the Tirpitz bombing

es mast- and 3,000 ft. e pillar

Air talks: 'Sufficient agreement'

GOEBBEL BOSS OF THE RUI

Several aspects

Turks have tripled chrome to Germany

3 A.M. LATE

JAPS SUN

Japanese ODESSA: 40,000

3 April: Operation Tungsten

The German warship *Tirpitz* was hidden in a Norwegian fjord when she was struck by successive waves of aircraft that had taken off from the carriers HMS *Furious* and HMS *Victorious* on 3 April. The *Tirpitz* was undergoing repairs and was caught completely by surprise; she was kept out of action for three months.

see Sinking of the Tirpitz p. 195

The *Tirpitz* is severely damaged by the Royal Navy.

5 April–22 June: Imphala and Kohima

On 6 March the Japanese launched their U-Go offensive in northern Burma. It planned to prevent the Allies taking Burma and to break through into India. British offensives had so far failed and the Japanese identified the border town of Imphala, which linked to the hill town of Kohima, as being the most promising line of attack. The Japanese 15th Army moved into Imphala at the same time as Slim was preparing for an offensive, but by 5 April the Japanese had cut the Imphala-Kohima road. Slim knew that it was imperative to deny the mountain roads down to the Indian Plain. Reinforcements were rushed to Kohima. The fighting began when 12,000 Japanese attacked the 1,200-manned garrison of Kohima.

Turning The Tide

By 7 April the situation was desperate; huge Japanese attacks took place between 17 and 18 April, but the Kohima garrison was relieved on 20 April. Fighting continued through May and at the end of the month the Japanese finally withdrew; Imphala itself was relieved on 22 June, after an 80-day siege. Of the 85,000 Japanese who had planned to invade India, only 20,000 were left. The Allies had suffered 17,857 killed, wounded or missing.

see War in China p. 91, and William Slim, p. 242

1936–45: Coastal Command

RAF Coastal Command was created on 14 July 1936. In total there were 19 squadrons, including six flying-boat squadrons. Their primary role was to patrol the North Sea, German-held coastlines, the northern Atlantic convoy routes and assist in the English Channel defence. They were also charged with making attacks on enemy U-boats and E-boats, performing air-sea rescues, protecting convoys and picking up the crews of sunken ships. Coastal Command played a leading role in the evacuation of Dunkirk. It was instrumental in spotting enemy vessels and was involved in the hunting of the Bismarck.

22 April–20 August: New Guinea

An 84,000-strong task force began landing in New Guinea on 22 April. They faced 11,000 Japanese defenders. The Japanese were heavily bombed prior to the landings and with the exception of protecting the airfields, the majority retreated into the mountains. Throughout late April and May more US troops landed in New Guinea and considerable progress was made. In the ensuing action, Japanese casualties reached 9,000, but the Japanese garrison, on Biak Island, remained defiant. The action developed on 29 May, with the first tank battle in the Pacific. Japanese resistance continued until 20 August.

see Saipan p. 168

US paratroopers.

9 May: Sevastopol is Liberated

After enormous resistance in the Crimea, the final pocket of German defiance began to crumble at Sevastopol. The last major thrust by the Russians began on 5 May and within four days the whole of the Crimea was in Russian hands. Small German rearguards held out for a further three days, covering the final German evacuation of the Crimea. In Moscow 24 salvos were fired from 324 guns to celebrate the victory.

1939–45: T34 Tank

The T34 tank ensured Russia's survival and Germany's defeat in the east, being capable of delivering devastating counterattacks to the German manouevres. Improvements to the T34-76 continued towards the end of 1941. T34s were instrumental in the Russian victory at Kursk (1943). Having achieved this, the Russians moved to produce the T34-85, which was an up-gunned version of the T34-76, with a different turret and a new five-speed gearbox. It mounted the M/39 85-mm gun which coped with German 75-mm and 88-mm tank and anti-tank guns. A new three-man welded or cast turret to house this weapon and mount it on a standard T34 chassis was proposed in an attempt to combat the increasing Panzers.

➧ see Soviets Launch Offensive Against Finland p. 167

25 May: Germans Attempt to Snatch Tito

In their continuing attempt to destroy or subdue Tito's Partisans in Yugoslavia, a crack German paratrooper force was dropped on to Tito's headquarters at Drvar in Bosnia. Tito and Major Randolph Churchill narrowly escaped capture. This was one of the Germans' last throws of the dice in Yugoslavia, as Russian troops would soon be in a position to link up with Tito's Partisans and push them out of the Balkans.

➧ see Tito Liberates Belgrade and Dubrovnik p. 191

JUNE

June 1944 will forever be remembered for the massive invasion of northern France, beginning with the D-Day landings on Normandy beaches on 6 June and continuing with the liberation of French towns and villages. Meanwhile the Russians were at loggerheads with the Finns, and set their sights for Minsk, while the war was turning against Japan.

1 June: Canaris is Dismissed as Head of the Abwehr

For several years Heinrich Himmler had been agitating to gain control of the German army military intelligence unit, the Abwehr, controlled by Admiral Wilhelm Canaris. By insinuation, Himmler had managed to implicate Canaris in plots against Hitler. Indeed, Canaris had been involved in the plots up to 1943, but as a result of his house arrest he was not involved in the July plot of 1944.

see Heinrich Himmler p. 234

Nazi Heinrich Himmler.

6 June: Operation Overlord

At 09:35 on 6 June the world was informed that the Allies had finally opened a front in France: 'Under the command of General Eisenhower, Allied naval forces, supported by strong air forces, began landing Allied armies this morning on the northern coast of France.' If anything the statement undersold the enormity of what had been planned. There were 1.7 million fighting troops in Great Britain by June, two million tons of war materials and 50,000 vehicles including tanks. They would be ranged against 500,000 Germans covering 1,287 km (800 miles) of coastline between Brittany and Holland.

Vast Armada

The blow would fall in Normandy, when a vast armada of 2,727 ships approached five designated beachheads, preceded by a parachute drop involving 20,000 Anglo-American troops and untold numbers of smaller commando and special-forces units striking at key positions in order to seize bridges or eliminate coastal defences. The sheer complexity of the operation beggared belief. The Channel had been turned into a vast, slowly moving stream of vessels, packed with troops and equipment, overflown by an overwhelming number of Allied fighters and bombers. Even as they landed, the Germans were convinced that this was simply a diversionary attack.

6 June: Airborne Landings and Raids

Landing in advance of the amphibious troops, were the British 6th Airborne and the American 82nd and 101st, totalling some 20,000 men. They dropped inland between St Mère Église and Carentan to support the US landings and to the east of the River Orne to support the Anglo-Canadian landings. Many would fall into swamp area, created by Rommel as an anti-invasion obstacle.

First French Village Liberated

The men were scattered far and wide by poor pinpointing of targets, yet 18,000 men succeeded in liberating St Mère Église (the first village in France to be liberated) and to seize control of the Caen Bridge over the River Orne. The Germans were caught entirely unprepared, but they were quickly able to deploy troops to oppose and block the movement of the paratroopers.

Chaotic Night

Nonetheless, it was a chaotic night and the paratrooper landings were often mistaken by the Germans as being diversions, feints, raids or attempts to seize senior German officers. Many of the paratrooper units would, nevertheless, have to hold or seize ground in order to assist their compatriots, driving off the beaches. No German dared wake Hitler, asleep in Berchtesgaden.

1940–45: The French Resistance

The French Resistance was created in the wake of a speech by Charles de Gaulle on 7 June 1940. The Resistance ranged from Socialists and Communists to ex-soldiers or Maquis. Many of the French Resistance were not French at all – they were either Spaniards, foreign nationalists, such as Britons or Americans, or other sundry individuals seeking to keep one pace ahead of the Gestapo. The Resistance used a cell structure in order to minimize their chance of being discovered. Primarily they were involved in helping Allied pilots who had been shot down. Occasionally they would launch attacks on isolated German positions but for the most part they were engaged in intelligence-gathering. From November 1940 the British Special Operations Executive sent in advisors and radio operators, as did the Secret Intelligence Service and the Special Air Service. Charles de Gaulle created his own group, the Bureau Central de Renseignements et d'Action (BCRA). The Resistance was constantly hounded by the Gestapo, the Wehrmacht and the Abwehr and, in Vichy France, the notorious Milice. The Resistance received an enormous increase in numbers in 1943 when the Germans initiated a forced labour draft. By that time the US Office of Strategic Services was operating in France.

Members of the French Resistance planning an operation.

6 June: D-Day Beaches

The Normandy landings took place along a stretch of the Normandy coast from Quinneville in the west to Ouistreham in the east. The two western beaches were designated as Utah and Omaha and were the concern of Bradley's 1st US Army. The three Anglo-Canadian beaches of Gold, Juno and Sword, were commanded by Dempsey. In overall command of the 21st Army Group was General Montgomery. American progress on their two beaches was comparatively slow and indeed the casualties were higher than expected on both beaches.

Allied troops land on the beaches of Normandy.

Juno and Sword

On the Anglo-Canadian beaches, however, the troops pushed rapidly inland, heading towards Bayou to the far west of the beaches and towards Caen inland. Unfortunately, the 21st Panzer Division quickly responded and blocked the junction of Juno and Sword beaches. By the end of the first day 155,000 men had landed on French soil. Rommel had always believed that if Germany had any chance of defending mainland Europe, then victory must be achieved on the beaches. In this he had lost the first and most vital battle. The pressure would grow until the break out became irresistible.

see Operation Overlord p. 161

1939–45: Sherman Tank

The Sherman was a remarkable US medium tank which fought in every theatre of the war in the service of every Allied army. The first Shermans were used by the British during El Alamein. Despite criticism about firepower and armour, the Sherman was cheap, easy to produce, rugged, reliable, had low maintenance needs and was fast. Some adaptations included the versions of the M4 with a rocket-projector rack mounted on top of the turret, commonly known as the 'Calliope', mine exploders, flail tanks, mine excavators, bulldozers, hedge-cutters and flamethrowers, as well as rocket launchers. These adaptations of the Sherman, from the M4 through to the M4A6, ceased production in June 1945, but the US army still used the Sherman in large numbers during the Korean War.

A US Sherman tank.

6–27 June: Stubborn German Resistance

By 8 June, in the face of growing German resistance, the British had managed to link up with the American beaches. The Germans still held Carentan, but pressure from the 101st Airborne cleared the town on 11 July. The Germans began counterattacking around Caen, halting the British drive on the town. By 12 June the US troops on Utah had still not reached the line of occupation they had meant to seize on the first day, yet assistance was on its way from Omaha beach. The British were able to punch through to Villers-Bocage by 13 June, whilst US troops attempted to cut off Cherbourg. Fighting was particularly intense around Caen and would remain so for a considerable time.

see Cherbourg Falls p. 170

Mulberry Harbours (1944)

One of the major problems choosing Normandy as the site for the invasion was the lack of immediate harbour facilities to bring in troops and equipment. The problem was solved in the most remarkable of ways. Vast floating concrete blocks, 60 m (197 ft) long, 18 m (59 ft) high and 15 m (49 ft) wide, were joined together to create two separate harbours, some 9.5 km (6 miles) in length. Further out to sea, nearly 60 obsolete merchant ships were sunk to form a breakwater. Remarkably, despite poor weather conditions, the Mulberry Harbours continued to be invaluable far beyond their intended period of use. The original design was by Professor Bernal who proposed it in 1943. The designs were developed by Brigadier Bruce White who created the final look for the Mulberry Harbours.

see Cherbourg Falls p. 170

6 June–2 July: Operation Neptune

Operation Neptune was the codename for the logistical movement of men and materials across the English Channel to the Normandy beaches. It was a vast undertaking and required a precision and coordination the like of which had never been attempted before. By 12 June some 326,000 men, 104,000 tons of war materials and 54,000 vehicles had made the

Channel crossing. By 2 July this had leapt to 929,000 men, 586,000 tons of equipment and 177,000 vehicles. This was the crucial phase of the operation. Operation Neptune did not end with the break out from the beaches and the pursuit of the Germans across France; by 15 August 1944 over two million men had crossed the Channel.

see D-Day Beaches p. 164

8 June: Soviets Launch an Offensive Against Finland

By 8 June the Russians and the Finns had still been unable to reach an agreement regarding disputed territories and alliances. Therefore, after a three-hour artillery bombardment, two Russian armies were pitted against the Finnish defence lines between Lake Ladoga and the Gulf of Finland to decide the matter once and for all. A truce was finally agreed on 19 September. The sticking point would remain Russia's reluctance to accept Finland's sovereignty.

see Finns and Soviets Agree a Ceasefire p. 183

A Mulberry Harbour, used in the D-Day landings.

10 June: Oradour-Sur-Glane Massacre

On 10 June groups from the SS Das Reich Division began rounding up the 652 inhabitants of Oradour-sur-Glane. They were told that they were suspected of hiding explosives and that the village would be systematically checked. The men were locked up in barns and the women and children in the church. The German troops then set fire to the village and shot anyone who tried to escape. Only 10 people survived the massacre.

➧ see Soviets Liberate the First Concentration Camp p. 176

15 June: B-29s Carry out First Raid on Japan

Having established relatively firm bases on mainland China, the US started to plan a periodic bombing campaign on mainland Japan. The US 20th Bomber Command had established several B-29 Super Fortress airfields and on 15 June carried out their first bombing raid on Japan. Their target was a steelworks factory at Jawata on Kyushu Island. In this first raid they managed to drop 200 bombs on target.

➧ see Tokyo Firebomb Raid p. 203

15 June: Saipan

Early on 15 June an enormous bombardment preceded the arrival of 700 landing craft, carrying elements of two US marine divisions on the west coast of Saipan. They faced 30,000 Japanese troops but managed to secure a beachhead 8.9 km (5.5 miles) wide and 1.2 km (0.75 miles) deep by the end of the first day. The Japanese launched a series of suicidal attacks during the night but were unable to dislodge the marines who were now firmly dug in. The Japanese continued to resist throughout June but by the end of the month their resistance in the south had ended. The island did not fall until 9 July, by which time 30,000 Japanese had died to the Americans 14,000.

19 June: The Marianas Turkey Shoot

Officially, at least, this engagement should be known as the Battle of the Philippine Sea: aircraft from nine Japanese aircraft carriers engaged those from 15 US aircraft carriers in the skies above the Marianas. The Japanese were also supported by aircraft from their nearby land bases. In near-suicidal attacks against the American fleet, the Japanese lost 400 aircraft in just one day, claiming 130 American planes. Battle continued into the next day, but, bereft of air cover, three Japanese aircraft carriers were obliterated, along with two destroyers and a fuel tanker. Ozawa, the Japanese commander, prudently decided to retire. The engagement is known as the Marianas turkey shoot due to the inexperience of the Japanese pilots.

see The Divine Wind p. 170

US battleships attack the Japanese at Saipan.

The Divine Wind (1944)

By 1944 the war had turned against Japan. Vice Admiral Takijiro Ohnishi, commander of the First Air Fleet, proposed setting up suicide units. The first was formed at Mabalacat airbase in the Philippines and included 26 pilots of the 201st Air Group, First Air Fleet of the Imperial Japanese Naval Air Force who joined the Kamikaze (Divine Wind) unit. Several such units were created and on 20 October the first 26 aircraft lifted off from Cebu airbase seeking out US vessels. They failed to find their targets at first but finally struck at Leyte Gulf, crashing into the aircraft carriers USS *Santee* and *Suwanee*. Other members of the group attacked the USS *Kitkun Bay* and the *St Lô*, the latter being sunk.

Kamikaze Missions

Kamikaze missions became an integral part of Japanese Air Force strategy. The suicide bombers were escorted by fighter aircraft to ensure they reached their targets. A new recruit had two week's flight training and a 10-day attack course; the best pilots were retained as escorts.

➧ see US Captures Saipan p. 174

23 June: Operation Bagration

In the summer of 1944 the Russians mustered 166 divisions to attack at six points in Belorussia; their final objective was the city of Minsk. They would face 38 depleted German divisions. Pivotal in this offensive was the Moscow–Minsk road and the Smolensk–Minsk railroad. Despite the fact that German intelligence had received notice of the attack, their defences were simply too weak to resist.

➧ see Soviets Liberate Minsk p. 172

27 June: Cherbourg Falls

By 20 June the pressure on Cherbourg was becoming intense and the following day the Germans were asked to surrender. No reply came. On 22 June, after an intense bombardment, the US launched their assault. Many German units instantly surrendered and by the following day the Allies were able to penetrate the outer defences. Fighting continued through 24 June and it became clear that it would only take one more push to gain control of the town. The German commander asked Rommel for permission to surrender. He replied 'in accordance with the Führer's orders, you are to hold out to the last round'. Cherbourg surrendered on 27 June.

➧ see Breakthrough at Caen p. 172

US troops enter Cherbourg.

JULY

Breakthroughs were now being made by the Soviets at Minsk and the British and Canadians at Caen, as the Americans pushed on through France. Japan continued to falter, with Saipan captured and Tojo relieved of his post. However, plots against Hitler failed and the Russians were faced with the remnants of the first concentration camp to be liberated.

3 July: Soviets Liberate Minsk

As the Russians marched into Minsk, the German Army Group Centre found 28 of its 40 divisions encircled. As a result of the fighting in the area, some 400,000 Germans had been killed, 158,000 taken prisoner, 2,000 tanks and 10,000 guns captured. What remained of the German front was now completely exposed. The Soviets had no difficulty in restoring liberty to the city.

see Warsaw Resistance Army Rises p. 178

8 July: Breakthrough at Caen

After many delays and false starts, early on 8 July, British I Corps launched its offensive against Caen, throwing three divisions against the city. The suburbs had been breached on 9 July, with the Canadian 3rd Division coming in from the west and the British 1st Division from the north. The 12th SS Panzer Division could do little to stop them. The following day a major offensive was opened south-west of Caen and by 11 July they had pushed 21 km (13 miles) to the west of the city. By 18 July the whole of the Canadian II Corps had crossed the Orne River and captured Colombelles and Giberville. The British VII Corps was engaged in a desperate struggle against the 1st SS Panzer Group to the south of Caen.

1940–45: The Fighting SS

The Waffen SS, or armed SS units, were created in 1940 and in most respects they can be differentiated from the SS-Totenkopfverbande ('death's head') units as they were primarily an elite military formation. By the end of the war some 600,000 men were serving in the Waffen SS, the fourth branch of the German Wehrmacht, although its control still remained within the hands of the SS. Waffen SS units would spearhead some of the most important battles of the war and were often given the most difficult combat challenges. They are, however, closely associated with innumerable war crimes, largely as a result of the political instructions and indoctrination given to them, rather than their prowess in battle. Waffen SS units invariably received the latest German equipment and were first in line for supplies, replacements and honours. Theoretically, there were 38 Waffen SS divisions, including the Leibstandarte Adolf Hitler, Das Reich, Totenkopf, Wiking and Hitlerjugend. Waffen SS units were primarily used for offensives but as the situation grew more critical they were increasingly deployed in a defensive role, rotated backwards and forwards between the east and western fronts.

see Operation Cobra p. 176

German SS troops.

9 July: US Capture Saipan

After ruinous combat since the middle of June, US troops finally reached Point Marpi on Saipan – the objective of their offensive – on 9 July. Only a handful at the Japanese garrison had been taken prisoner and at Point Marpi the marines discovered the grisly atrocity left by the Japanese. They had systematically thrown hundreds of civilians over the cliffs to their doom.

see Guam p. 175

US marines during the capture of Saipan.

18 July: Tojo is Relieved of his Command

The loss of Saipan was the final straw for the Japanese government. They had relied on Tojo to guide the country to victory, but on 18 July he was relieved as Chief of General Staff and replaced by General Yoshijiro Umezu. The following day the Japanese government resigned and Emperor Hirohito asked General Koiso to form a new government.

see Hideki Tojo p. 244

20 July: July Plot

An elaborate anti-Nazi plot sprang into action on 20 July 1944. The plan involved the murder of Hitler, Goering and Himmler. Von Stauffenberg placed a bomb in Hitler's conference room, which succeeded in killing four people, but only injuring Hitler. Other conspirators would seize Berlin and eliminate Goering and Himmler. Hitler survived and the plotters were rounded up, tortured and slowly executed. Around 4,980 Germans were executed as a result of the plot.

see Adolf Hitler p. 234

21 July–10 August: Guam

After a massive air and naval bombardment, the 3rd Marine Division and elements of the 77th Infantry Division began landing on the west coast of Guam in the Marianas at 08:30 on 21 July. They were quickly able to establish a beachhead 3 km (2 miles) wide and 1.6 km (1 mile) deep. They faced 12,000 Japanese under Takashima's command. On 25 July the Japanese launched seven attacks and lost 3,500 men. By 28 July Takashima was dead and US marines had reached the edge of the airfield. By 1 August half the island was in US hands and Japanese resistance ended on 10 August, having suffered at least 15,000 casualties. US forces, despite overwhelming firepower, had suffered 1,400 casualties.

see US Land at Leyte p. 192

24 July: Soviets Liberate the First Concentration Camp

Russian troops discovered what was left of the Majdanek concentration camp on 24 July. The camp had been in operation since February 1943 and around 130,000 Jews had been slaughtered there, in addition to Polish prisoners and Soviet prisoners of war. It has been estimated that around 200,000 people perished in this camp altogether. Several thousand inmates were still alive amongst the dead when the camp was liberated.

25 July: Operation Cobra

The much-awaited breakout from the beaches of Normandy was achieved by the sheer weight of German troops being attracted into the Caen area to deal with the British and Canadian forces in action there. This left the American 1st Army with the comparatively simple task of punching through towards St Lô. Codenamed Operation Cobra, the offensive was masterminded by General Bradley. He had thought carefully and at length about the operation. Cobra started on 25 July with thousands of Allied aircraft undertaking an aerial bombardment of a limited area, designed to destroy defences and create a breach through which Bradley's troops could move. Due to a lack of German troops and materiel, it was impossible for them to offer

General George Patton.

much in the way of resistance to the advancing US troops. Even so, there were the remnants of a German defensive line, and so progress was slow on the first day, but by 27 July the VII and VIII Corps had made a complete breakthrough. By the following day, US troops were advancing southwards on the west bank of the River Vire to the east of St Lô. The operation was a success, and the Americans were able to move out of Normandy, towards the Seine and on to the ultimate goal: Paris.

Patton Takes Command

On 30 July the Germans launched a massive counterattack, which temporarily held off the advancing Americans. On the first day of August, General Patton assumed command of the US 3rd Army and was given the job of holding the extreme right of the Allied line. On 5 August his units approached Brest and St Malo, while other units were pushing deep into Brittany. Brest was a key Allied target, as it was vital to secure the capture of ports in northern France to enable the planned invasion of Europe to take place. Elements of Patton's army reached the outskirts of Brest in the evening of 7 August and the following day the Germans were asked to surrender. The request was met with a point-blank refusal.

1943–45: Patton's Corps

George Patton was an archetypal cavalry commander, born perhaps 100 years after his time. Nonetheless, he swiftly adapted to the concept of commanding tracked vehicles and fast-moving columns of troops in numerous campaigns from 1943. His corps had been involved in the original Torch landings in 1943 and had shown considerable dash in their race across Sicily in order to beat Montgomery to Messina. When Operation Overlord was launched, Patton's troops were not landed in France until August but were then placed exactly where Patton could do the most damage. With the British holding the Germans down at Caen, it wasn't long before he found the roads of France open and swept virtually unopposed through the countryside, helping to hasten the defeat of the Axis powers in the west.

➧ see The Falaise Gap p. 179

AUGUST

Ground was now being consistently gained against the Germans, most importantly in France where the Allies pushed on from the south and the north, ultimately leading to the liberation of Paris. However, an uprising in Warsaw found it could not count on Soviet support until it was too late, and the Frank family lost their struggle to avoid discovery and deportation.

1 August: Warsaw Resistance Army Rises

In eager anticipation of the imminent arrival of Russian troops, Polish patriots staged an uprising in Warsaw, hoping their presence would ensure an independent post-war Poland. For political reasons, Russian troops advancing on the city paused in the suburb of Praga on the opposite side of the Vistula River. They waited until the Polish resistance army had been surrounded and wiped out by the Germans before they continued their advance.

Women of the Warsaw Resistance.

4 August: Soviets Reach Baltic Sea

Facing increasing pressure, the German Army Group North temporarily managed to hold off Russian attempts to capture Riga. On 1 August the Russians had captured Kaunas, the capital of Lithuania. The German attack reopened the Estonian-Latvian corridor between Riga and the Russian salient at Jelgava, the end of a 724-km (450-mile) supply line.

4 August: Arrest of Anne Frank and Her Family

Anne Frank was born on 12 June 1930. After the Nazi invasion of Holland, she and her family and four other Jews sought refuge in a few rooms above her father's office in Amsterdam, in an effort to avoid being deported to one of the many concentration camps that had been built as labour or extermination camps. They were under constant threat of discovery but she was betrayed in August 1944 after spending 25 months in hiding. She was arrested and deported to a concentration camp. She died in Bergen-Belsen in March 1945 at the age of 15. Her diary, which she kept during her period of hiding, described her everyday life and her fears. The diary survived the war and has been translated into 55 different languages.

15 August: Operation Dragoon-Anvil

Operation Dragoon-Anvil was the codename for the Allied landings on the south coast of France, involving 2,000 transport and landing craft, escorted by 300 warships. In one day, 94,000 men were landed and established a solid beachhead. A German attack ended in failure with the loss of 15,000 men and 4,000 vehicles. By the end of August some 48,000 prisoners had fallen into Allied hands.

see Operation Overlord p. 161

16–20 August: Falaise Gap

On 16 August Canadian troops entered Falaise, whilst the British I Corps moved towards the River Seine. To the south US forces had reached Dreux and Chartres. Almost trapped around Falaise were the German 5th Armoured Army and the 7th Army, amounting to some 250,000 Germans. The Falaise Gap was sealed on 20 August and within the pocket a fearful slaughter began, with Allied aircraft ranging at will across the battlefield, destroying any German tank or vehicle that came into sight.

Allies Advance

The German troops who had been defending German-held France for so long were now trapped and the Allies showed little mercy until every formation and unit was ready to offer unconditional surrender. Their loss hastened the end in the west and with it the fall of Paris. The Allied forces were now advancing towards the borders of Germany itself. German losses included 200,000 prisoners and at least 50,000 deaths. Some 240,000 men had managed to break through at various points, but these reached the safety of the German lines with little more than the clothes on their backs.

The bomb-wrecked city of Falaise, as it was found by the Canadian troops in 1944.

1941–45: Typhoon Tank Buster

It was cannon fire from a Hawker Typhoon fighter bomber of 266 Squadron that effectively took Field Marshall Rommel out of the war, when it swooped on his staff car in Normandy in 1944. Rommel was so seriously injured that he played no further part in command operations. The Typhoon had its maiden flight on 26 May 1941 and it came into service the following September. The Typhoon had originally been thought of as a successor to the Hurricane, but it was in its ground-attack role, particularly after D-Day, that it came into its own. The RAF had 26 squadrons of these aircraft, which had a maximum speed of 641 kph (398 mph). During the Battle of Normandy the Typhoons accounted for 137 tanks around Avranches. In total 3,330 Typhoons were built.

15 August: Liberation of Paris

On 19 August an uprising arose in Paris against the German occupation. There was bitter street fighting, but already the French 2nd Armoured Division was moving towards Paris and on 23 August the US 4th Division entered Arpajon, to the south of the city. By 24 August Leclerc was close to the south-western suburbs of Paris and running into some difficulties. The US 4th Division was ordered to attack from the south and two bridgeheads were secured over the River Seine. At 07:00 on 25 August Leclerc's troops entered Paris from the south-west and half an hour later the US 4th Division broke through in the south.

Civilians and troops celebrating the liberation of Paris.

Paris Surrenders

The German commander, in defiance of Hitler's orders to raze Paris, surrendered the city. Liberation officially occurred at 15:15. The following day the Canadians headed towards Calais, while the British thrust towards Belgium and the US 1st Army began moving along the Paris–Brussels Road. German troops were still holding out in Brittany and Brest still defied the Allies. On 28 August Leclerc continued his advance north-east and Allied troops aimed to cross the River Somme.

› see Liberation of Brussels p. 183

SEPTEMBER

While the Soviets pursued their objectives, agreeing a ceasefire with the Finns and declaring war on Bulgaria, the Allies enjoyed successes in France and Belgium, anticipating action to be taken in Holland and Germany during Operation Market Garden, an initially successful and yet ultimately failed attempt to get to the heart of Germany's industry.

Troops being welcomed by citizens of Liège.

3 September: Liberation of Brussels

The provisional French government transferred back to Paris on 31 August, while Allied troops established a bridgehead over the River Meuse, near Verdun. On 1 September Verdun was liberated and the Canadians reached Dieppe. Advances were already being made towards Metz. On 2 September the US 1st Army had almost reached the Belgian frontier, while the British advanced towards Le Havre. The following day Brussels was liberated by XXX Corps. The next day the British unit took Antwerp.

Series of Allied Successes

On 5 September the Allies enjoyed a series of successes: Boulogne was taken; the Meuse was crossed at Sedan; and the Moselle near Nancy. The following day Liège was also liberated and the outskirts of Bruges were reached on 8 September.

› see German and Dutch Borders are Crossed p. 185

4 September: Finns and Soviets Agree a Ceasefire

On 2 September the new Finnish Prime Minister, Antti Hackzell broke off diplomatic relations with Germany. Two days later the Finns requested a ceasefire and an armistice was agreed between the Finnish and the Russian governments. On 6 September the Finnish delegation arrived in Moscow to discuss the armistice.

5 September: Soviets Declare War on Bulgaria

On 5 September the Russians declared war on Bulgaria and sent their troops across the border within hours of the declaration. They had barely got underway when Bulgaria surrendered. On 7 September Bulgaria declared war on Germany and they agreed to allow occupation by Russian troops. Four Russian armies, one motorized corps and one air army entered Bulgaria to take over the occupation.

› see Soviets Push into Prussia p. 191

8 September: V2 Rocket Hits London

The V2 rocket, or Vergeltungswaffe ('reprisal weapon 2'), was a vast early attempt at an intercontinental missile. In truth it had a limited range, and had been built at the slave-labour camp of Dora, near Nordhausen in Germany. The first battery to reach operational stage had intended to fire on Paris, but after several launch failures, rockets were fired from the vicinity of Houffalize and The Hague on London.

➧ see German Rocket Programme p. 197

Bomb damage on a London street.

9 September: German and Dutch Borders are Crossed

The US XIX Corps reached the Maastricht area on 9 September, crossing the borders of Belgium and Holland. The push towards Antwerp was postponed due to the imminent Operation Market Garden. By 11 September the entire French Channel coast, with the exception of Boulogne, Calais and Dunkirk, was in Allied hands. On the same day, units of the US 1st Army crossed the German border near Aachen, creating panic amongst the locals.

17 September: Operation Market Garden

Operation Market Garden was launched on Sunday 17 September and involved the dropping of a carpet of paratroopers throughout Holland to the Rhine, with a view to securing key bridges to enable an encircling of Germany's industrial heartand, the Ruhr. The British 1st Airborne Army would be dropped in and around Arnhem, with the task of capturing the bridges over the lower Rhine. The US 101st would land to the north of Eindhoven and the 82nd would land near Grave to the south of Nijmegen. They would hold the vital bridges until such a time as Horrock's XXX Corps could push up through the corridor and reach Arnhem. The British paratroopers found powerful German forces on the ground around Arnhem and only a portion of the force managed to break through to the Arnhem Bridge.

Key Objectives

The 101st managed to take its objectives and held the bridges over the Wilhelmina and Zuiter Willemsvaart Canals. The 82nd, meanwhile, managed to capture the bridge at Grave, but were denied the Nijmegen Bridge due to heavy German opposition. XXX Corps managed to join up with the 101st to the north of Eindhoven on 18 September, but German troops were being rushed in increasing numbers to the area. Despite initial successes, Operation Market Garden failed to fulfil the hopes of a 1944 end to the war.

» see Red Devils p. 186

1942–45: Red Devils

Although late in creating airborne troops, the British had in their paratroopers some of the finest soldiers, capable of carrying out missions from small raids to enormous operations. Whilst they were deployed in advance of amphibious landings in Normandy, it is Operation Market Garden that established their immortality. Three divisions landed along a narrow stretch of Dutch countryside to secure the bridges which the British XXX Corps needed to drive to Arnhem. Following intense fighting the paratroopers fulfilled all obligations except taking the southern end of Arnhem Bridge.

1942–45: US Airborne Forces

The 82nd Airborne was the first US airborne unit. It was earmarked to spearhead the landings for Operation Husky and its objective would be to seize and hold the high ground above the beaches in Sicily that would be used by Patton's Divisions. The 82nd was then used for the Salerno landings in September 1943 and again for Operation Overlord in June 1944. The 101st Airborne, known as the Screaming Eagles, were created in August 1942. They first saw action during Operation Overlord and were an integral part of Operation Market Garden. Their finest hour, however, occurred over Christmas 1944, when they held Bastogne against German attempts to seize the crossroads to Antwerp. Elements of the division were surrounded on 21 December, but they refused to surrender, forcing the Germans to bypass them. The Germans launched their last assault before dawn on Christmas Day, but elements of the 4th Armoured Division came to their timely rescue.

17 September: The Arnhem Landings

The British paratroopers who had managed to reach the Arnhem Bridge were cut off and German troops were massing all around the British perimeter. By 19 September it was obvious that the rest of the paratroopers could not break through to Arnhem. On 21 September the paratroopers dug in on the north bank of the Rhine to the west of Oosterbeek, determined to hold out until XXX Corps reached them. By now those at the

Arnhem Bridge had been overwhelmed. In desperation, Polish paratroopers were dropped to the south of the Rhine and Eindhoven, but they could not cross the river to link up with the British paratroopers. On 26 September, 2,200 of the original 10,000 men managed to re-cross the Rhine to safety.

17–25 September: Nijmegen

The seizing of the bridges at Grave and Nijmegen were the responsibility of the 82nd Airborne. Paratroopers were dropped either side of the Grave Bridge, but at Nijmegen this did not happen as it was considered that the Groesbeek Heights, a plateau some 91 m (300 ft) above the bridge, was more important. The priority became to capture the heights before an attempt was made on the bridge itself. As a result, the Nijmegen Highway Bridge was not taken, allowing the Germans to send troops across to hold back XXX Corps. The bridge was finally taken in a breathtaking attack by troops in assault groups across the Waal River. The paratroopers lost half of their force, but 200 of them established a bridgehead, allowing the capture of the bridge.

➧ see Operation Market Garden p. 185

Allied tanks crossing the Nijmegen bridge.

17–25 September: Eindhoven

Initially the 101st met with little resistance and captured the bridge at Veghel. Significantly, however, German anti-tank guns held off the 101st long enough for the Son Bridge to be destroyed. The 101st had only one other option – to capture the bridge at Best – but they could not break through. Efforts were then concentrated on moving south to reach the northern end of Eindhoven. By noon they had linked up with advanced units from XXX Corps. By the evening XXX Corps were in Eindhoven, camped to the south of the wreckage of the Son Bridge while they awaited the arrival of the Royal Engineers to build the bridge.

Bailey Bridge

On 19 September the Germans made a determined attack to destroy the Bailey Bridge before it had been built. They were beaten back by increasing numbers of XXX Corps. By the time XXX Corps were in a position to cross, the Germans had positioned heavy units on either side of the road, making an advance towards Arnhem suicidal. By 23 September XXX Corps were a few kilometres from Arnhem, but another German force moved to block the road.

› see XXX Corps p. 258

21 September: The Polish Landings

On 21 September, 1,000 Polish paratroopers dropped to the south of the Rhine. A further 500 had been held up in Britain due to poor weather conditions. The Poles made straight for a ferry across the Rhine, intending to relieve the British airborne troops. Unfortunately the ferry had been destroyed. The Poles, under Sosabowski, tried everything they could to secure a crossing of the Rhine, but each attempt met with failure. They were on hand to cover the evacuation of the exhausted British troops when they could finally leave. On 22 September they attempted a last crossing of the river by attaching boats to a signal cable. It was unfortunately spotted by the Germans and only 52 Poles had managed to cross.

1942–45: Me262

The Me262 was a revolutionary turbojet engine aircraft, originally designed by Messerschmitt in 1938. It first flew on 18 July 1942, but the Luftwaffe was cautious and there were developmental problems with it. By late 1943, Hitler had insisted that the aircraft be introduced as a fighter-bomber, but it was not until 25 July 1944 that the first Me262 was used in combat, when one attacked a British aircraft over Munich. The Me262 was deadly as a fighter/interceptor against the vast streams of Allied bombers over Germany, but in fact, of the 1,400 built, only around 300 saw combat. By this stage the German Luftwaffe was lacking spares, trained pilots and sufficient fuel to commit large numbers to the air.

see Operation Bodenplatte p. 200

1944: XXX Corps

Horrocks's XXX Corps faced the task of getting 30,000 vehicles along one road to Arnhem in just three days. XXX Corps had fought as a unit in North Africa, Sicily and mainland Italy, before being transferred back to Britain in preparation for Operation Overlord. They had fought on the beaches in Normandy and then across France into Belgium and were now poised on Dutch soil waiting to thrust the dagger into Germany's heart. Although three parachute divisions had been dropped along the corridor and massive artillery and air bombardment had taken place either side of the road, there were still considerable numbers of hidden German units ready to ambush the column. The most difficult situation occurred at Eindhoven, where one of the vital bridges had been destroyed. It took 36 hours to construct the Bailey Bridges. XXX Corps were ultimately blamed for not pressing forward with the required speed, but even when failure was imminent, Horrocks was still determined to press on and reach Arnhem.

Brian Horrocks.

see Brian Horrocks p. 235

OCTOBER

In October, the Allies made some patchy headway in Germany, Eastern Europe and the Philippines, but it was another bloody month for all concerned, with the Germans fiercely resisting and the Japanese ever more persistent in their kamikaze attacks.

1–21 October: Battle of Aachen

On 1 October the US 1st Army began its operations aimed at surrounding Aachen. After an artillery and air bombardment, US forces began advancing between Aachen and Geilenkirchen on 2 October. By the next day they had penetrated the Siegfried Line and had been caught up by the 2nd Armoured Division. On 4 October the Germans launched a counterattack to close the gap, but by now the American V Corps was preparing to enter the action. On 5 October the road to Aachen was cut off and vicious German counterattacks took place around Metz.

US Ultimatum

On 10 October the US 1st Division delivered an ultimatum to German troops in Aachen, ordering them to surrender. The ultimatum expired unanswered the following day and the assault was resumed. The bombing and shelling continued into 12 October and on the 13th the Americans

Wreckage surrounding the cathedral of Aachen after the battle.

prepared for their final assault. Street fighting continued for a number of days but by 20 October the Germans only held the southern suburbs. Finally, at 12:05 on 21 October, after the city had been reduced to rubble, the German garrison surrendered.

see Battle of the Bulge (Ardennes Offensive) Begins p. 195

15 October: Athens is Liberated

On 14 October the British 3rd Corps and a number of Greek units were poised to land at Piraeus. Their landing was temporarily held up by mines in the harbour. On the previous day British Commandos and Greek troops had landed near Piraeus and occupied the Kalamata airfield. British troops entered Athens on 15 October, determined to deal with the Greek insurrectionists who were already in control of the city.

see Tito Liberates Belgrade and Dubrovnik below

18 October: Soviets Push into Prussia

The major Russian offensive against East Prussia – begun on 18 October – was met by strong German resistance, but the Russians had already penetrated Czechoslovakia and on 20 October the Germans were driven out of Debrecen in Hungary. On 21 October the Russians reached the River Danube and the following day they managed to break through the defences in East Prussia but were halted at Insterburg. For the rest of the year the front in this sector would remain unchanged. Operations were continuing in Romania, however, and the Russians had now occupied Transylvania. In Hungary, by 26 October, the front had stabilized along the River Tisza. By 1 November Russian troops were close to Budapest.

see Soviets Reach Budapest p. 197

20 October: Tito Liberates Belgrade and Dubrovnik

On 16 October vicious fighting broke out in Belgrade between Tito's Partisans and the Germans. To the south the Russians had occupied Nish. By 18 October Belgrade was on the point of falling into Partisan and Russian hands as Army Group F began to retreat from the Balkans. On 20 October Belgrade was liberated and Tito's Partisans managed to capture Dubrovnik.

20 October: US Land at Leyte

At 10:05 on 20 October, the lead units of some 120,000 men began landing on the east coast of Leyte Island in the Philippines. MacArthur himself was in overall command. He reminded the Filipinos of his promise to return. The invasion force would face 260,000 Japanese deployed across the islands. On 21 October Japanese suicide attacks were beaten off and the following day US troops moved inland.

23–25 October: Battle of Leyte Gulf

From the outset of this bitter battle, there were huge casualties to both the US and Japanese fleets. At 05:32 on 23 October the *Atago* became the first casualty, swiftly followed by the *Maya* at 05:54, both victims of US submarines. At 08:30 on 24 October the USS *Princeton* was hit by enemy aircraft and was finished off by her own ships that afternoon. Between 10:27 and 19:35 the Japanese battleship *Musashy* was hit by several torpedoes and eventually sank. The battle was rejoined the following day with opposing destroyer flotillas engaging. The Japanese battleship *Fuso* was sunk at 04:18 and later in the day, after both sides had suffered destroyer losses, the Japanese heavy cruiser *Suzuya* sank at 13:22.

Disastrous Engagement

Once again the fleets locked horns on 25 October; there were more destroyer losses but the Americans had found three Japanese aircraft carriers. At 09:37 the aircraft carrier *Chitose* was hit and sunk; 14:14 the *Zuikaku* capsized, joined at 15:26 by the pulverized *Zuiho*. Leyte Gulf was a disastrous engagement for the Japanese. In the follow-up actions, which lasted until 27 October, they would lose three more light cruisers to US submarines.

25–29 October: Kamikaze attacks on Leyte Gulf

The Battle of Leyte Gulf and its aftermath were marked by an enormous number of kamikaze attacks on US vessels. The worst occurred on 25 October, when land-based aircraft attacked the USS *Santee*, the USS *Suwannee* and the USS *St Lô*. All were hit by suicide aircraft, the latter sinking at 11:15. Five minutes previously the USS *Kalinin Bay* had also been badly damaged.

Suicide Pilots

Wave upon wave of Japanese aircraft appeared over the US fleet, oblivious to the anti-aircraft fire and US fighters. Their sole intention was to immolate themselves on the decks of the enemy vessels. The suicide pilots managed to damage seven escort carriers, one light cruiser, eight destroyers, two landing craft and a tanker during the battle.

Troops on the beach at the Battle of Leyte Gulf.

NOVEMBER AND DECEMBER

November saw the completion of the notorious Burma 'Death Railway' – only to be repeatedly bombed by the Allies. It also saw the longed for sinking of the *Tirpitz* and the liberation of many parts of the Balkans. Then in December, the long and crucial battle for control of Antwerp began.

November: Burma-Siam Railway Opens

During November the final sections of the notorious Burma-Thailand railway were completed. The railway stretched some 400 km (249 miles) and it was said that each of the sleepers along its track marked the resting place of one of the Allied prisoners of war or convicts from Southeast Asia who had died during the construction project. The total body count has been estimated at 150,000.

The German battleship *Tirpitz* sinks.

12 November: Sinking of the Tirpitz

By August 1944 the *Tirpitz* had completed its sea trials. It immediately came to the attention of the Allies, who desperately wanted to sink it. The operations codenamed Goodwood and Paravane failed or were only partially damaging, but it was not long before Operation Catechism was launched on 12 November, when 32 Lancaster bombers appeared over the *Tirpitz* at approximately 09:35. The vessel finally went down with 1,000 of her 1,700 crew; the Lancasters suffered no losses.

➧ see Kriegsmarine p. 25

29 November: Liberation of Albania

On 20 November the Germans evacuated the Albanian capital of Tirana. On 29 November they evacuated Scutari and moved to link up with Army Group E, which was attempting to hold open the withdrawal route. The evacuation of Albania and Serbia was quickly followed by Bosnia and Herzegovina, with the Germans digging in from Bisegrad, across to the River Drina and to Mostar.

➧ see Soviets Capture Vienna p. 210

16 December: Battle of the Bulge (Ardennes Offensive) Begins

Originally the last major push by German forces in the west had been fixed to take place on 27 November, but with the latest news, Hitler agreed that it should be postponed until 16 December. With great secrecy and skill the Germans managed to assemble a force of 30 divisions, 2,000 guns, 1,000 tanks and 1,500 aircraft. The divisions alone included 250,000 men. The primary objective was to punch a hole straight through the US lines and effectively cut off the British army advancing in the north. It was imperative the Germans deny the Allies the opportunity to take the Antwerp port. Once the harbour was clear of mines, men and equipment could be brought into the city without having to take the tortuous route through France.

Intricate Operation

For the operation to succeed, each phase would have to be minutely timed. The offensive was also planned to take full advantage of poor weather conditions, eliminating Allied air supremacy. The route the attack would take had been used in 1940 to push the Panzer divisions around the flank of the Maginot Line and it was for this reason that the Ardennes was chosen. The forested area would also provide cover for the German armoured columns. The attack relied on speed, the capture of fuel and no hold ups. Unfortunately for them, the first push to reach the River Meuse and open the road into Belgium, led by Kampf Gruppe leader Joachim Peiper on 16 December, almost immediately fell behind schedule after discovering that a vital bridge had been destroyed. He then encountered US opposition; Peiper's men were caught in a pocket near La Gleize on the afternoon of 18 December and virtually destroyed. Nevertheless, by 20 December, German troops had pushed a considerable distance into US-held Belgium and Luxembourg. The high point of the offensive came when the 2nd Panzer Division arrived within range of Dinant on the River Meuse; however, by 20 January the Germans would be back at their starting point.

see Joachim Peiper p. 240

Joachim Peiper.

17 December: Malmedy Massacre

Elements of the 1st SS Panzer Division approached the Baugnes crossroads near Malmedy, Belgium, encountering a company of the US 7th Armored Division. The US commander, realizing the odds against him, ordered his men to surrender. The troops were searched, marched into a field and shot. Eighty-six were killed, over 40 survived.

20–27 December: Siege at Bastogne

Bastogne lay at a vital crossroads and in the path of several German Panzer divisions and supporting units. It was effectively surrounded by the night of 24 December, yet despite intense pressure, the hastily scraped together defenders refused to surrender. Bastogne was defended by the 101st Parachute Division and elements of the 9th and 10th divisions under McAuliffe. Patton came to their aid after intense bombardment and attacks on the position.

see Allied Counteroffensive in Ardennes p. 201

27 December: Soviets Reach Budapest

By 26 December Russian troops had closed off the avenue of escape from Budapest and by 27 December the final stages of the battle for the city had begun. Desperate street fighting continued throughout the city until 13 January 1945 when it was taken by the Russians. The armistice was signed and Hungary declared war on Germany on 21 January.

see Soviets Capture Warsaw p. 201

1944–45: German Rocket Programme

Werner von Braun worked on a series of designs which would culminate in the creation of the V2 rocket, the first of which was fired at London on 8 September 1944 (the first of some 1,358). Other British targets included Norwich and Ipswich, while Antwerp received 1,610. Expensive and too primitive to hit specific targets, the V2 was militarily ineffective. The far more effective machine was the V1, or Buzz Bomb (Doodlebug), of which 30,000 were manufactured, a third of which were fired at Britain. They were difficult to shoot down but experienced pilots could tip them off target to land harmlessly in the sea.

see Werner von Braun p. 227

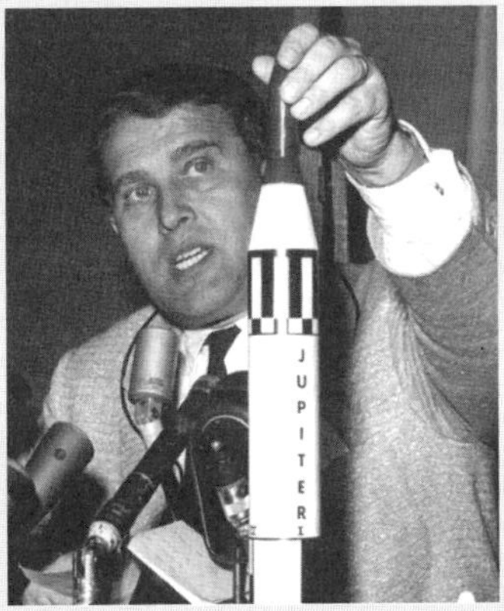

Wernher von Braun with a model of his rocket.

220
1415
1265

1945

JANUARY

The Luftwaffe's surprise attack on Allied airfields, Operation Bodenplatte, took place on New Year's Day. In the Pacific, the Battle of Luzon began this month, as part of the US ongoing defence of strategically important Philippines. The Allies launched a counteroffensive in Ardennes, in order to push back the German advance in the area. By the end of the month, Warsaw had been taken by the Russians.

1 January: Operation Bodenplatte

Operation Bodenplatte was a bold surprise initiative taken by the Luftwaffe on New Year's Day 1945. Somehow the Luftwaffe had scraped together 800 aircraft, mainly bombers. The majority were flown by inexperienced pilots, but the targets were Allied airfields in France, Belgium and Holland. The offensive took the Allies completely by surprise, and between 150 and 300 Allied aircraft were lost, mainly on the ground. Irreplaceable Luftwaffe casualties amounted to some 200.

➧ see Dresden p. 203

1943–45: Chafee

The M24 Chafee was a successor to the M5 Stuart light tank. It saw service with the US army's reconnaissance and light-tank battalions throughout Europe and in the Pacific and was also supplied to the British army, who nicknamed it the 'Chafee'. The M24 was considered to be a reliable, manoeuvrable and fast vehicle and would not only be one of the first western Allied tanks to cross the Rhine, but also would still be in use during the Korean War, and remained in many armies throughout the world for a number of years after the war.

➧ see Bridge at Remagen p. 205

9 January: Marines Land on Luzon

Early on 9 January, after a vast air and naval bombardment, some 67,000 US troops began landing in the Gulf of Lingayen on the west coast of Luzon. They would face 262,000 Japanese under General Yamashita. The handful of Japanese aircraft made little headway, except for damaging the USS *Mississippi* and the cruiser USS *Columbia*. But the Japanese navy deployed kamikaze boat pilots and managed to sink an American transport ship.

see US Liberates Manila p. 202

9–16 January: Allied Counteroffensive in Ardennes

The US 1st and 3rd Armies were charged with the task of dealing with the salient created by the German Ardennes counteroffensive. All units made good progress and by 16 January the Ardennes salient was half its former size. Continued pressure continued until 20 January, when the Germans found themselves where they had started over a month previously. Meanwhile, Patton's 3rd Army was advancing on every front and reached the junction of the Rivers Sauer and Our. On 21 January a new Allied offensive in the St Vith area was planned; this time the weather had improved and there would be good air cover. The Ardennes offensive cost the Germans 100,000 casualties, 1,000 aircraft and 800 tanks. Allied losses were in excess of 80,000.

17 January: Soviets Capture Warsaw

The Russians allowed the Polish 1st Army to launch the final offensive against Warsaw. Very few people had managed to live among the ruins and after the Warsaw uprising the Germans had deported 600,000 people to concentration camps. By 18 January the last Germans had been driven from Warsaw and the Russians began their advance out of Poland and towards the German border.

The capture of Warsaw.

FEBRUARY

Early February saw the US liberate Manila, and the battle to occupy the strategically important island Iwo Jima began. The Yalta Conference, at which plans for the post-war world were drawn up, took place between Churchill, Stalin and Roosevelt. Allied air attacks were carried out over Dresden and Tokyo.

3 February: US Liberates Manila

Elements of the 1st Cavalry Division managed to reach the outskirts of Manila, supported by the 37th Division on 3 February. On 5 February the last of the Japanese began to withdraw from the northern outskirts of the capital and MacArthur ordered his men forward to seize the city. Cleaning-up exercises continued for a number of days and Japanese counterattacks were repulsed.

4–11 February: Yalta Conference

At the Yalta Conference, Churchill, Roosevelt and Stalin reached agreement on the remaining war strategy and the post-war world. Russia agreed to turn against Japan as soon as Germany had been conquered. Although the two western Allies were concerned about the power Stalin might wield in the post-war years, they had little choice but to concede further allowances in the Far East to him in order to ensure his support.

› see Unconditional German Surrender p. 215

Churchill, Roosevelt and Stalin at the Yalta Conference.

13–14 February: Dresden

Late on 13 February a formation of 244 Lancaster bombers began dropping incendiaries on the major German city of Dresden. Three hours later, a larger force hit Dresden again. The city was aflame, but on 14 February a vast armada of US B-17 bombers dropped tons of high explosives on the shattered city. The Germans claimed 70,000 had perished in the bombings (later reappraised at 250,000). Allied estimates, based on Russian figures, placed around 320,000 dead, although more contemporary evidence puts the figure at no more than 35,000.

➧ see Raid on Bershtesgaden p. 210

19 February–26 March: Iwo Jima

Iwo Jima was a tiny island, but an important asset for whoever could control it – from here bombers could rain terror on the Japanese mainland. The Japanese had mustered 22,000 men for its defence and they had spent months building strong points and bomb-proof positions. Landings commenced on 19 February and from the outset met heavy opposition from the Japanese. By the end of the first day the marines had taken over 2,000 casualties, but they had cut the island in two. Although the US flag was raised on Mount Suribachi on 23 February, the battle was by no means over. Fresh American reserves had landed and by 11 March the last Japanese survivors were holding Kitano Point at the island's northernmost tip. Of the 22,000 Japanese only 212 were captured; the rest had been killed. US dead and wounded had topped 26,000.

➧ see Okinawa p. 208

25 February: Tokyo Firebomb Raid

The US Air Force XXI Bomber Group, flying B-29 Super Fortresses, carried out a devastating firebomb raid on Tokyo on 25 February. Around 170 aircraft dropped incendiary bombs on the largely wooden capital of Japan. A square mile of the city was devastated. On the same day carrier-born aircraft precision bombed Japanese airfields and aircraft factories. The procedure was repeated the following day, again over Tokyo.

➧ see Tokyo Air Raid p. 206

MARCH

This month saw the Allies begin to take a position of ascendancy over the enemy, as strategic targets in Germany were taken, including Cologne and the Rhine area. In the Pacific theatre, the Allies struck Tokyo in a devastating air raid.

Collapse of the Remagen bridge.

7 March: Bridge at Remagen

The same day that the US 3rd Armored Division captured Cologne, elements of the 9th Armored succeeded in establishing bridgeheads across the Rhine and the Ahr. The most stunning coup of the day was the capture of the Remagen Bridge. It had been the American intention to destroy the bridge and cut off German troops trapped west of the Rhine. However, seeing it intact made them change their operational plans and they immediately threw troops across the bridge, switching their whole axis of attack.

Hitler Furious

News of the disaster reached a furious Hitler, who immediately sacked von Rundstedt (Commander-in-Chief of German forces in the west). Hitler said of von Rundstedt 'He is finished. I don't want to hear any more about him.' Kesselring was recalled to take up the position. Over the next two days some 300 Luftwaffe bombers attempted to destroy the bridge, but they failed. By now thousands of Allied troops had crossed the Rhine and were taking up strong positions in the newly gained bridgehead. By 11 March cleaning-up exercises to the west of the river were all but over.

1945: The Pershing

The Pershing tank received its baptism of fire at Remagen on 7 March. The tank saw limited service during the war but it was well matched against the best of the German tanks. It had arrived in the European Theatre too late to have any significant impact; however, in the summer of 1945 it was deployed against the Japanese on Okinawa. The Pershing remained in US military service and saw considerable action during the Korean War. At last the US had created a tank which was the equal of any other vehicle in either the Axis or Allied armouries. Had it been available earlier, it would have made a significant impact on the progress of the war.

➧ see Operation Varsity p. 206

9 March: Tokyo Air Raid

In a combined operation, 334 B-29 bombers, flying out of Guam, Saipan and Tinian, launched a three-hour incendiary bomb raid on Tokyo on 9 March. Ten square miles, a full fifth of the total area of the city, was razed to the ground. Japanese sources admitted to 130,000 dead, although other figures suggest it could have been as high as 200,000. If the Japanese had thought conventional weapons were devastating, the worse was yet to come.

see Japanese Government Collapses p. 209

Extensive bomb damage in Tokyo after the B-29 raids.

24–25 March: Operation Varsity

On the morning of 24 March, an enormous air armada of 3,000 aircraft and gliders passed over the River Rhine and began dropping 14,000 paratroopers of the British 6th Airborne and the US 17th Airborne Division. The armada took 2.5 hours to pass over the Rhine; it was supported by nearly 900 US and RAF fighter aircraft. The paratroopers were dropped around Wesel, with instruction to link up with the British 2nd Army forces. By the evening they had captured all their key objectives and had penetrated 10 km (6 miles) into German territory.

Allied Supremacy

The operation had been meticulously planned and was, in many respects, exactly what Arnhem should have been. By this stage German troops were increasingly unable to respond rapidly to any growing danger, due to the immediate interdiction from Allied air superiority. By 26 March the airborne units had extended their area of occupation and were advancing rapidly. By 29 March elements of the 2nd British Army had reached Osnabruck.

Dortmund-Ems Canal

By early April XXX Corps had managed to reach the Dortmund-Ems Canal. British forces were closing their side of a vast salient that had developed in the Ruhr, which was being exploited by the US 1st Army.

APRIL

This was a month of high drama, during which the war in Europe rapidly span out of German control, the Japanese government collapsed, the Allies discovered the existence of the concentration camps in Germany and Mussolini was assassinated. Hitler retreated to a Berlin bunker, but by the month's end he, along with many of his inner circle, was dead.

1 April: The Ruhr Pocket

By 1 April, with Canadian troops having advanced beyond Osnabruck, elements of the British army linked up with the US 9th and 1st Armies at Lippstadt, effectively closing off the Ruhr region. The whole of Army Group B and two corps of the 1st Parachute Army were trapped in a 113-km (70-mile) pocket located between the Rivers Rhine and Ruhr. The pocket stretched 80 km (50 miles) from the River Sieg to the River Lippe. Over the next couple of days the British added their weight to the offensive and the Americans consolidated their position. On 4 April pressure was applied from both the north and the south and a new offensive was opened two days later.

Collapse of German Front in Italy

By 14 April the bulk of the pocket had been pierced and 325,000 Germans were taken prisoner, held in transit camps for German POWs known as *Rheinwiesenlager* (Rhine meadow camps). The German commander, Field Marshal Walther Model, had sworn to Hitler that he would fight to the death, and committed suicide rather than surrender. By now, events were overtaking issues on the Ruhr; western Allied thrusts had passed Hanover and Leipzig and the German front in Italy had collapsed. In the east the situation was worse and within days both Vienna and Berlin would fall and Hitler would be dead.

➧ see Allies Meet on the Elbe p. 211

1 April–22 June: Okinawa

US intelligence believed that the garrison on Okinawa was 65,000-strong but it was in fact double this figure. The job of taking the island fell to the 10th Army and its 180,000 men. The main landing on 1 April was preceded by a huge bombardment and during this time the Japanese launched 193 kamikaze missions against the fleet. Regardless, the US was able to land 60,000 men on the first day. The island was fanatically defended and as the Americans advanced, the Japanese launched a series of costly counterattacks. The main Japanese defence lines were pierced on 24 April but they ran into a second line of defence four days later.

The beachhead at Okinawa.

Kamikaze Attacks

Throughout April more kamikaze missions were launched and by the end of the month over 3,000 of these attacks had been made; the US had lost 21 ships as a result. On 21 May the Japanese began to fall back from their last defence line, but it was not until 22 June that the last resistance was crushed. Indeed Okinawa was not secure until 2 July. The Japanese had lost 107,500 killed and significantly, 7,400 taken prisoner.

› see Allies Deliver an Ultimatum to Japan p. 220

5 April: Soviets Denounce the Pact with Japan

With the war in Europe rapidly spinning out of German control, the Russian government informed the Japanese Ambassador in Moscow that they intended to denounce their five-year non-aggression pact, which had been signed in 1941. Stalin had already moved considerable military assets east in order to exploit Japan's worsening position in the Pacific and the imminent US attacks on their mainland.

› see Soviet Union Declares War on Japan p. 222

5 April: Japanese Government Collapses

The Japanese battleship Yamato, sunk in the East China Sea.

Facing the threat of Russia as well as Britain and the US, the government of General Kuniaki Koiso realized it was finished. Koiso resigned and a new government was formed under Admiral Kantaro Suzuki. On 7 April, the Japanese attacked the US in the battle of the East China Sea. The Japanese ships were overwhelmed and the *Yamato* was sunk.

see US Plans to Invade the Japanese Mainland p. 217

11–13 April: Allies Liberate Buchenwald and Belsen

In their offensive into the Weimar sector the US 3rd Army stumbled on Buchenwald and Bad Sulza, two extensive German concentration camps. On 13 April, as British troops drove towards Bremen and sought to cross the River Leine, they crossed the Luneberg Heath and discovered the Nazi concentration camp at Belsen. At Belsen the British found 40,000 prisoners on the verge of death and thousands of rotting corpses. Even after the liberation, around 600 died every day. At Buchenwald the US troops rushed food and medical supplies to the 20,000 survivors. Thousands more of them would die within days of liberation.

see Dachau is Liberated p. 213

13 April: Soviets Capture Vienna

After seven years of German occupation, Vienna fell to Russian troops on 13 April after several days savage fighting. Ironically, the last German stand in Vienna was in the old Jewish quarter. Their choice of this location saved many of Vienna's most important historic buildings. At the end of the fighting the Russians had netted 130,000 prisoners. On 15 April, Hitler uselessly bragged 'Berlin is still German, Vienna will return to Germany'. Already the Russians were preparing for the final push on Berlin and had amassed 1.6 million men, 3,827 tanks, over 2,000 self-propelled guns, 4,500 anti-tank guns, 15,500 field guns, 6,700 aircraft and 96,000 other vehicles. To oppose these the Germans had just 47 divisions.

see Allies Meet on the Elbe p. 211

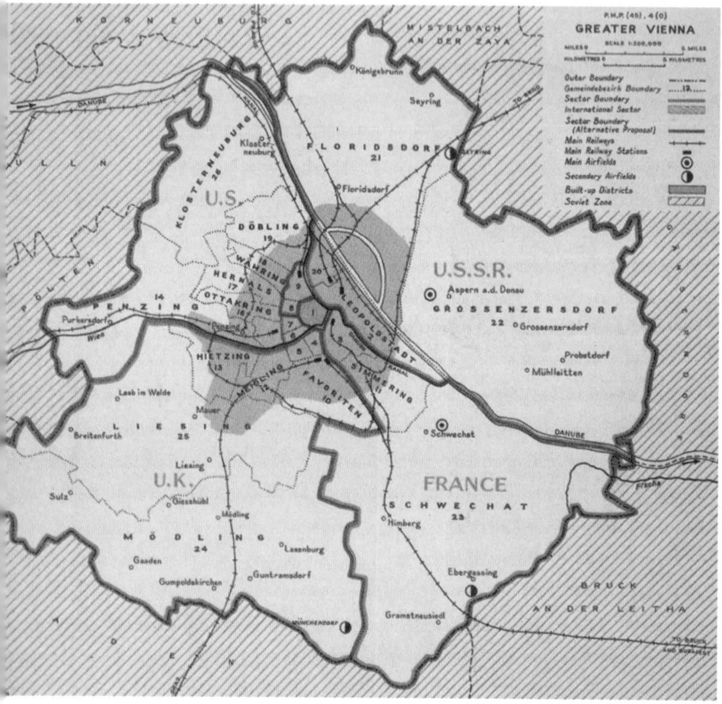

Map showing Allied occupied zones.

24 April: Raid on Bershtesgaden

The RAF Bomber Command launched their last major operation against Hitler's mountain residence of Bershtesgaden on 24 April. They failed to catch Hitler there, but ironically only one day before, after six years, the blackout in London was lifted. Hitler had officially taken over the defence of Berlin. He was in charge of 300,000 men and women whom he exhorted to defend the capital to the very last.

see Food not Bombs p. 212

25 April: Allies Meet on the Elbe

As Anglo-American and Russian troops cut through Germany, they first met at Torgau on the River Elbe. To the north US troops were reaching Russian lines on the Baltic coast. Across Germany white flags hung from windows and the Allies were having difficulty dealing with the number of refugees, not to mention the one million German prisoners captured by the western Allies alone in the last three weeks.

see Doenitz Takes Control p. 214

26 April: Pétain Fails to Escape to Switzerland

Pétain had been arrested by the Germans on 20 August after refusing to stand down. He had been taken to Belfort, but on 1 October he was removed from there and taken to Sigmaringen in Germany. On 26 April Pétain was arrested attempting to cross the Swiss border from France. Subsequently he was tried for treason and sentenced to death – later commuted to life imprisonment.

see Mussolini and his Mistress are Assassinated p. 212

Marshal Pétain.

28 April: Food not bombs

In response to the privations being suffered in Holland, notably a grave shortage in food, US B-17 Flying Fortresses and RAF Bomber Command Lancasters appeared over the cities of The Hague, Rotterdam and other major centres. On this occasion their cargoes did not rain death, but instead contained vital food parcels and medical supplies for the starving Dutch. By May food was routinely being brought into Holland by truck.

see Unconditional German Surrender p. 215

28 April: Mussolini and his Mistress are Assassinated

Mussolini and his mistress, Clara Petacci, were arrested and tried by the partisans on 28 April. Mussolini was found hiding under a pile of coats in a convoy of cars. He immediately surrendered and after a brief trial was condemned to death. The sentence was immediately carried out along with his mistress and 12 other fascist leaders. Their bodies were taken to Milan where they were hung up on display.

29 April: Hitler and Eva Braun Marry

Determined to remain in Berlin until the bitter end, Hitler gave orders that the struggle should continue in southern Germany in what he believed to be an alpine fortress. His major act of the day, however, was to marry his long-term mistress, Eva Braun. They wed in a bunker beneath the shattered streets of Berlin.

Hitler and his mistress Eva Braun at their Bavarian retreat.

29 April: Dachau is Liberated

Several different US army units claim to have liberated the Dachau concentration camp. What is certain was the impact of seeing thousands of starving prisoners and thousands more dead; a line of cattle trucks alone contained the bodies of over 2,300 Hungarian and Polish Jews. SS Guards were treated roughly and it has been suggested that up to 500 of them were executed on the spot by vengeful US troops.

see Post-War Legacy p. 246

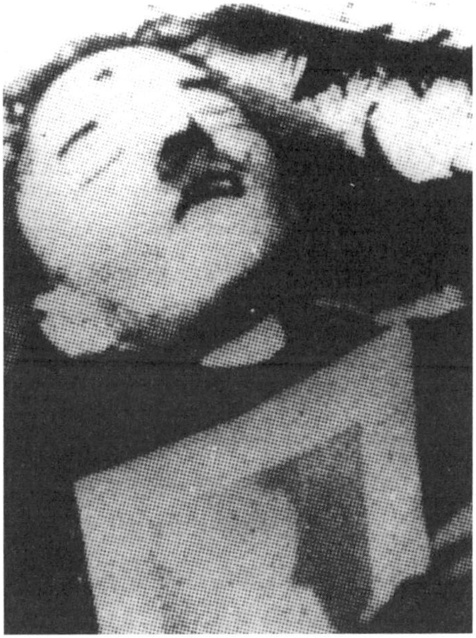

30 April: Hitler Commits Suicide

At approximately 15:30 on 30 April, Adolf Hitler committed suicide, having taken the life of Eva Braun, whom he had married just the previous day, prior to turning the gun on himself. He had given up hope that any German troops would be able to save Berlin. Indeed, that night advanced units of the Russian 150th Infantry Division stormed the Reichstag and planted the hammer and sickle on its roof.

Hitler shot his wife of one day, Eva Braun, before committing suicide.

Hitler's Inner Circle Dies

There was mass panic in the Führer bunker and Goebbels had his whole family killed before taking his own life. Many of the inner circle either jockeyed for position in the dying embers of the German empire or simply disappeared. Key figures such as Himmler and Goering would later be picked up, but others, including Bormann were never positively identified.

see Doenitz Takes Control p. 214

MAY

In May 1945, after nearly six years of war, the Allies at last claimed victory in Europe. The Italians and Germans surrendered unconditionally, and the conflict in Europe was over. The war in the Far East, however, was far from over, with the US making plans to invade the Japanese mainland.

1 May: Doenitz Takes Control

On 1 May, the official announcement of Hitler's death reached the German public. He had appointed Doenitz as his legal successor. Grand Admiral Karl Doenitz, speaking on Hamburg radio, assured the German people that the struggle would go on. In truth few Germans believed him as the situation was worse than critical. In effect there was no longer an Eastern and Western Front; they had merged into one and small groups of German units now concentrated on trying to struggle westward in order to avoid falling into the hands of the Russians. There was no more chance of defending the soil of Germany when the prospect of a Siberian labour camp beckoned. Doenitz had his own plans for Germany.

see Karl Doenitz p. 229

Grand Admiral Doenitz.

1 May: Fall of Berlin

As over a million German troops began surrendering in Italy and Austria, General Krebs, the senior German officer in Berlin, was told by the Russians to accept unconditional surrender. At this stage both Bormann and Goebbels were alive and determined to continue the struggle, but General Weidling, the garrison commander, decided on a surrender. Bormann disappeared, whilst Goebbels and his family and Krebs committed suicide. The order to surrender went out to Berlin but still-fanatical Nazis continued to resist within the city. The following day Russian troops concentrated on clearing opposition in the capital and isolated pockets of resistance still remained.

2 May: Germans Surrender in Italy

The German situation in Italy had become untenable and Colonel Schweinitz, representative of General Vietinghoff signed an unconditional surrender, effective from 13:00 hours on 2 May 1945. The surrender document encompassed all German troops under his command in Italy. On the same day, however, US troops reached Milan, which had already been liberated by anti-fascist Partisans. The following day Turin fell.

3 May: Rangoon is Liberated

On 1 May the British launched Operation Dracula and two Gurkha parachute battalions were dropped on the mouth of the Irrawaddy River to the south of Rangoon. On 3 May they linked up with the 20th Indian Division advancing down the Irrawaddy Valley. The Japanese evacuated Rangoon just as the 26th Indian Division liberated the city. There were, however, still some isolated Japanese troops to be dealt with in Burma.

» see US Plans to Invade the Japanese Mainland p. 217

4 May: Unconditional German Surrender

On Doenitz's instructions, General von Friedberg signed the unconditional surrender document at 18:20, authorizing the capitulation of all armed forces in Holland, north-west Germany and Denmark. The document was signed at General Montgomery's headquarters at Luneberg Heath. The full surrender took place at 02:41 in a schoolhouse in Rheims, when

Field Marshal Wilhelm Keitel signs the surrender to the Red Army on 9 May 1945.

Jodl, the German army Chief of Staff, signed the full unconditional surrender document before General Eisenhower. Jodl commented 'With this signature, the German people and the German armed forces are, for better or for worse, delivered into the victor's hands.'

Victory At Last

The Germans had delayed the full surrender to allow as many of their troops to struggle westward as possible. The real surrender had occurred with the signature at Montgomery's headquarters, but now this unconditional surrender had been made in the presence of the representatives of Britain, Russia and the US. Across Europe the relief was almost tangible. After six years of war, the privations were temporarily forgotten in a blaze of fireworks and flags.

see Goergy Zhukov p. 245

18–26 May: Chinese Take Foochow and Nanning

In the Fukien Province, Chinese forces reoccupied Foochow and additional Chinese divisions, engaged and fighting in Burma, began moving back towards China on 18 May 1945. On 26 May the Japanese evacuated Nanning, the capital of Kwangsi Province. This meant that the Japanese no longer had an overland communication route with Indo-China. On 7 June the Chinese launched a major operation to assist in liberating Hong Kong and Canton.

22 May: British Capture Himmler

Himmler was arrested in Bremen on 22 May, disguised as a German military policeman. He was taken into immediate custody and was due to stand trial with other prominent Nazi leaders as a war criminal at Nuremberg, but he had secreted a cyanide capsule which he took before his British captors could interrogate him. Even to his death Himmler remained an unrepentant Nazi.

see British Capture Von Ribbentrop p. 218

25 May: US Plans to Invade the Japanese Mainland

On 25 May the US military began consideration of the proposed invasion of the Japanese mainland. A series of documents were produced between May and June. Over the previous six months 300,000 Japanese had been killed during bombings. The Joint Chiefs of Staff set the invasion of Kyushu (Operation Olympic) for 1 December 1945 and the island of Honshu (Operation Coronet) for 1 March 1946.

24–26 May: Tokyo is Firebombed

On 24 May 520 American bombers dropped 3,500 tons of bombs on the centre of Tokyo and industrial areas to the south. The bombers were back on 26 May; this time they dropped 3,252 tons of bombs on the Ginza district and areas adjacent to the Imperial Palace. By this stage Japanese war production was down to 20 per cent.

see Allies Deliver an Ultimatum to the Japanese p. 220

JUNE AND JULY

As many of the chief German architects of the war were rounded up for trial by the Allies, the conflict in the Far East continued with the Allies delivering Japan an ultimatum in late July. In Britain, Winston Churchill lost the election to Clement Atlee, who took charge of a new, post-war government.

10 June: British Capture Von Ribbentrop

Von Ribbentrop was captured by British troops on 10 June. He was one of the key figures being sought by the Allies. As it transpired at Nuremberg, he was active in the planning of the attack on Poland, the framing of the Final Solution and conspiracies ending in the murder of Allied prisoners of war.

see Joachim von Rippentrop p. 241

Joachim von Ribbentrop.

1 July: Chinese Keep up the Pressure

On 1 July the Chinese liberated Liuchow and on 27 July they began a month-long battle for the possession of Kweilin. Meanwhile, on 5 August the Chinese 13th Army captured Tanchuk and the 58th Division, Hsinning. By 12 August it was clear that the Japanese were on the verge of surrender and consequently the Chinese decided to cancel their intended invasion of Hong Kong and Canton.

see Soviet Union Declares War on Japan p. 222

5 July: Churchill Loses the Election

The results of the 5 July General Election in Britain were declared on 26 July. It was a landslide victory for the Labour Party with 393 seats against the Conservative's 213. Churchill was shaken by the result. He was quoted as saying 'The decision has been recorded. I have therefore laid down the charge which was placed upon me in darker times. It only remains for me to express my profound gratitude for the unflinching support they have given their servant through these perilous years.' The new Prime Minister, Clement Attlee, said of the victory 'We are facing a new era. Labour can deliver the goods.' By 27 July Attlee was in the thick of it at the Potsdam Conference.

see Potsdam Conference p. 220

The new British Prime Minister Clement Attlee, who defeated Churchill.

16 July: First Atomic Bomb is Detonated at Los Alamos

On 16 July, at 17:30 at Los Alamos in New Mexico, the first atomic bomb was successfully detonated. The project to develop the weapon had been completed by an international team of scientists. Within a matter of days an additional weapon would be created that would hasten the end of Japan's resistance.

see Manhattan Project p. 220

Manhattan Project (1942–45)

In the 1930s it became clear that the Germans were working on an atomic bomb. In the US the major effort to create an atomic bomb got underway in 1942. Whilst the Manhattan Project continued apace, British special-operations executive agents managed to destroy a vital factory in Norway that the Germans needed to build their bomb. The Germans quickly rebuilt it and in November 1943 it was destroyed once again, this time by American bombers. The first of three US bombs was tested at Los Alamos, New Mexico on 16 July 1945.

➧ see Hiroshima p. 221

17 July-2 August: Potsdam Conference

Central to the discussions between Churchill (soon to be Attlee), Truman and Stalin at this conference was the situation in Europe and possible solutions to end the war against Japan. There was disagreement about the territorial boundaries of Germany. Stalin refused to allow free elections in Eastern Europe and brushed aside criticisms of the situation in many of these countries. It was Churchill who coined the term 'Iron Curtain', as he felt that Stalin was excluding the West from all decisions related to Eastern Europe.

Churchill, Truman and Stalin at the Potsdam Conference.

26 July: Allies Deliver an Ultimatum to the Japanese

During the Potsdam Conference the Allies issued a proclamation demanding Japan's unconditional surrender, rather than face 'prompt and utter destruction'. Japan formally rejected the Potsdam ultimatum on 30 July. Meanwhile conventional warfare continued with increasingly desperate kamikaze attacks on US shipping near Okinawa. The US responded by bombarding airfields and industrial targets across Japan. The US attacks continued until 1 August then ceased.

➧ see Hiroshima p. 221

AUGUST

The situation in the Far East was brought to a dramatic head with the dropping of the war's first atomic bomb on Hiroshima in Japan. The Soviets declared war on Japan, due to the latter's breaking of a non-aggression pact between the two nations. After a second atomic bomb was dropped, this time on Nagasaki, Japan accepted an unconditional surrender.

6 August: Hiroshima

On 6 August a B-29 bomber dropped the first atomic bomb on a live target. The bomb, equivalent to 20,000 tons of high explosive, flattened the city of Hiroshima in Japan. More than 92,000 people were killed instantly, some 37,400 more injured, many of whom would die agonizing deaths over the next decade and more. The decision to drop the bomb had not been an easy one, but Truman saw this as a means to avoid a potentially ruinous invasion of Japan. Japan had been trying to seek a negotiated peace, but it could not accept unconditional surrender as this would impact upon Emperor Hirohito.

Choosing the Target

The choice of target had also been difficult to make. Originally the favoured target was Kyoto but due to its historical importance Hiroshima had moved to the top of the list. Truman issued the order to drop the bomb on 25 July after the US army's strategic airforces in the Pacific requested a written authorization.

The atomic bomb on Hiroshima.

1945: B-29

The B-29 was the most expensive weapon created by the US during the war. Some 4,000 were used in the Pacific alone. They were mass-assembled in various US cities including Seattle, Washington and New Jersey. Today only one airworthy B-29 Super Fortress remains in existence, although several are being restored.

8 August: Soviet Union Declares War on Japan

The successful dropping of the first atomic bomb on Hiroshima made the future seem bleak for the Japanese – they had no weapon that could match the destructive power of that now wielded by the Allies. But there was worse to come. The Russians, having repudiated their non-aggression pact with Japan on 5 April, stepped up the pressure by declaring war.

9 August: Nagasaki

On 9 August the US B-29 Great Artist dropped a second atomic bomb on Nagasaki, a major ship-building centre. In seconds, between 25,000 and 70,000 people were killed and a further 43,000 injured. Truman had given the sternest warning 'If they do not now accept our terms, they may expect a rain of ruin from the air, the like of which has never been seen on this earth.' Churchill was more philosophical and said, in a statement read by Attlee, 'By God's mercy, Britain and American science outpaced all German efforts... The possession of these powers by the Germans at any time might have altered the result of the war.'

14 August: Japan Accepts an Unconditional Surrender

With great reluctance, Emperor Hirohito accepted an unconditional surrender. He recorded his message on the 14th and, after an attempted coup d'état at the Imperial Palace to prevent him doing so, managed to broadcast it to the nation the next day. The US received the news and prepared to begin the occupation of Japan. However. the news took some time to filter through to Japanese combat units and it was several days before mass surrenders began to take place.

SEPTEMBER–NOVEMBER

September saw the signing of the official unconditional surrender of the Japanese. In November, the Nuremberg trials began, with the key Nazi figures appearing in front of a military tribunal. The trials lasted until October 1946.

2 September: Japanese Surrender Ceremony

Aboard the USS *Missouri* anchored in Tokyo Bay, the Japanese Foreign Minister and Chief of Staff, Woshijiro Umezo, signed the unconditional surrender document at 08:00 in the presence of General MacArthur. Clement Attlee spoke at midnight in Britain saying 'Japan has today surrendered. The last of our enemies is laid low.' Truman addressed the crowds from the White House and said 'This is the day we have been waiting for since Pearl Harbor'.

see The Post-War Legacy p. 246

Japan signs an unconditional surrender to the Allies.

20 November–October 1946: Nuremberg Trials

Twenty-two of the key Nazi figures were tried by an international military tribunal at Nuremberg from 20 November. The tribunal had representatives of the British, Russian, American and French governments. The Nazis were all charged on four counts: conspiracy to wage war; crimes against peace; war crimes; and crimes against humanity. Some did not have their sentence carried out. Goering would cheat the hangman by swallowing poison. Rudolf Hess would commit suicide in prison in 1987 and von Neurath served just eight years of his sentence.

see The Post-War Legacy p. 246

PERSONALITIES

PROTAGONISTS AND ANTAGONISTS

From ill-fated Chamberlain to people's hero Churchill, from chilling Himmler to passionate dictator Mussolini, the key protagonists and antagonists of the war formed part of a greater human effort led by many thousands of men on all fronts.

Alexander, Harold (1891–1969)

Major-General Harold Alexander commanded the 1st division of the British Expeditionary Force when they went to France in 1939. It was Alexander's men who covered the retreat and evacuation at Dunkirk. He was then sent to Burma, but was unable to stop the Japanese. After a short time he took command in Egypt and worked with Montgomery in forging the victory in North Africa. It was Alexander who organized the attacks on the Gustav Line and Monte Cassino in particular. After the war Alexander became the Governor General of Canada and then served as Minister of Defence under Winston Churchill. He died on 16 June 1969.

British commander Harold Alexander.

Auchinleck, Claude (1884–1981)

General Auchinleck was put in command of Allied troops in the Middle East in July 1941. That November he launched Operation Crusader against the Axis forces in North Africa. The campaign initially appeared successful, but the following May Rommel launched a counteroffensive. Auchinleck was outmanoeuvred and large numbers of Allied troops were lost. He was replaced on 8 August 1942. Auchinleck later took command of British forces in India and became a full Field-Marshall. He was forced to resign in August 1947 (accused of being pro-Pakistani at this crucial time), but he remained in the army until his retirement in 1968.

Braun, Werner von (1912–77)

In 1937 Braun and Walter Dornberger (the man in charge of rocket research for the German army) began developing long-range missiles, which eventually led to the creation of the V2. From September 1944 onwards, over 5,000 V2s were fired at Great Britain. By March 1945 the launch sites had been overrun and Braun fled west and surrendered to US forces. He was shipped to the US to work on the nuclear programme. In 1952 he became the technical director of the US Ballistic Missile Agency and in 1960 the director of Marshall Space Flight Center. He resigned in 1972 and died on 16 June 1977.

Chamberlain, Neville (1869–1940)

Neville Chamberlain.

Chamberlain came to power as Prime Minister in 1937. His policies allowed the Anschluss, the union of Germany and Austria in 1938. When Hitler demanded control of German-speaking Czechoslovakia (Sudetenland), Chamberlain signed the Munich Agreement, on 29 September 1938. With this, it seemed that war had been avoided, but in March 1939 Hitler seized the rest of Czechoslovakia and Chamberlain realized that Hitler could not be trusted. When German troops rolled across the Polish border in September 1939, Chamberlain was forced to declare war. He proved to be an inept war leader and was eventually replaced by Winston Churchill.

Chiang Kai-Shek (1887–1975)

At the time of the Japanese invasion (1937), China was ruled by the Nationalists, led by Chiang Kai-shek. The invasion forced Chiang to join forces with Mao Tse-tung, the Communist leader, to combat the Japanese. In 1941 Chiang's army received support from Joseph Stilwell, commander of the US forces in China, Burma and India, but Stilwell and Chiang disagreed on many issues. The arguments caused the recall of Stilwell in October 1944. After the collapse of the Japanese and a ruinous civil war the Communists gained control of China. Chiang and what remained of his army established an opposing regime in Taiwan. He died in April 1975.

Chinese General Chiang Kai–shek.

Churchill, Winston (1874–1965)

Following a successful British army career, Churchill became a war correspondent before being elected as an MP. By 1933 his extreme views on rearmament and his opposition to Hitler's Germany caused his fall from favour in the government, but despite uncertainty about his methods and beliefs, Prime Minister Neville Chamberlain appointed Churchill First Lord of the Admiralty in April 1940. A month later Chamberlain resigned and Churchill was asked to form a government.

Churchill's leadership kept Britain afloat in the early war years and he became something of a hero-figure. He developed a strong relationship with the Unites States, and after the attack on Pearl Harbor in December 1941, Churchill worked closely with Roosevelt to ensure victory over the Axis Powers, welcoming Russia on board to develop a united strategy. After the war Churchill lost power in a landslide Labour victory, but returned in 1951. He retired in 1955 due to ill-health and died on 24 January 1965.

Free French leader Charles de Gaulle.

De Gaulle, Charles (1890–1970)

De Gaulle was a French soldier who by May 1940 was a major tank commander. In June he was appointed Minister of War, but when Pétain assumed power de Gaulle was sentenced to death and fled to England. Until 1943 he sought to unite the French resistance and formed the French Committee of National Liberation. In August 1944 de Gaulle's 2nd Armoured Division entered Paris. On 13 November 1945 de Gaulle was officially recognized as head of the French government. From 1946 de Gaulle continued to adopt right-wing policies, seeking to regain French power and independence. He retired in 1969 and died on 9 November 1970.

Doenitz, Karl (1891–1980)

By 1935 naval officer Doenitz had taken control of the German U-boat fleets. Lacking sufficient submarines, he carried out widespread attacks on Allied shipping between 1940 and 1943. Doenitz became head of the German navy (1943), but the naval war had turned against Germany and the battle for the Atlantic was lost. Despite increasing submarine production from 1943, German naval forces' resistance had collapsed by 1945. Hitler appointed Doenitz his successor just before committing suicide. Doenitz negotiated Germany's surrender on 8 May, was tried at Nuremberg, and received 10 years imprisonment. He was released in 1956 and later died on 24 December 1980.

Grand Admiral Doenitz.

Air Marshal Sir Hugh Dowding.

Dowding, Hugh (1882–1970)

Dowding served as the commander of 16 Squadron of the Royal Flying Corps during World War I, joining the newly formed Royal Air Force in the interwar years, and being promoted to Air Marshal in 1933. He was instrumental in the development of the Spitfire, Hurricane and radar, and ultimately took over control of Fighter Command. Dowding successfully argued that the development of fighter defences was imperative in the impending war against the German Luftwaffe, and his tactical abilities led to victory in the Battle of Britain. He formally retired in July 1942 and died in February 1970.

Eisenhower, Dwight D. (1890–1969)

Eisenhower was sent to Britain as leader of the European Theatre of Operations in March 1942, and was given command of Operation Torch, the Allied landings in north-west Africa. Later, as a full General, he began organizing the invasion of Italy. He was then given the responsibility of organizing three million troops for the full invasion of Europe as Head of Supreme Headquarters Allied Expeditionary Force. He retired in 1948, but became Supreme Commander of NATO in 1951 and on 20 January 1953 became President of the United States. Eisenhower died at Gettysburg on 28 March 1969.

Gibson, Guy (1918–44)

Gibson joined the RAF in 1936, winning the Distinguished Flying Cross in July 1940. In 1942 he was promoted to Wing Commander and flew 172 missions as Commander of 106 Squadron, before being posted as Commander of 617 Squadron. On the night of 16 May 1943, Gibson led 19 Lancasters on the successful attack on the Ruhr dams. He was awarded the Victoria Cross for his role in the mission. On 14 September 1944 he flew a Mosquito fighter bomber on a raid against German targets in Holland. He and his navigator were killed when their aircraft crashed over enemy territory.

Joseph Goebbels reviewing his troops in Berlin.

Goebbels, Joseph (1897–1945)

Goebbels was the intellectual of the Nazi Party who helped sweep them to power in 1932. Hitler appointed him Reich Minister for Public Enlightenment and Propaganda, giving him complete control of the media. Goebbels was a strong supporter of the 'Final Solution' and directed the deportation of Berlin's Jewish population in 1942. Goebbels saved Hitler and the Nazi regime in the aftermath of the July 1944 attempt to assassinate Hitler by rounding up the conspirators. To the end, he remained Hitler's most loyal follower, choosing death for himself, his wife and six children in the Berlin bunker on 1 May 1945.

Goering, Hermann (1893–1946)

As Commander-in-Chief of the Luftwaffe, Goering led campaigns against Poland and France. The Luftwaffe began their assault on Britain in August 1940, as a prelude to the planned invasion. They failed, however, and Hitler never forgave Goering. From 1943 the Luftwaffe came under increasing pressure, reduced as it was to defensive operations against the growing air power of the Allies. Goering was arrested after attempting to seize the reins of power in Germany. He was captured by US troops in May 1945, tried at Nuremberg and found guilty on four counts of war crimes. He committed suicide on 5 October 1946, two hours before his scheduled execution.

Hermann Goering.

Graziani, Rudolfo (1882–1955)

Before the outbreak of World War II Graziani was the Vice-Governor, then Governor, of Cyrenaica and Libya. He later served as the Governor of Somalia and the Viceroy of Ethiopia. From 1939 to 1941 he was the Italian Chief of General Staff, while simultaneously serving as the Governor General for Libya and the Commander-in-Chief for Italian forces in North Africa. Mussolini effectively sidelined him after his defeat but he returned as the Minister of War for the Socialist Republic of Italy after Mussolini had been deposed. At the same time, he served as the General Commanding Officer of the Ligurian Army.

Guderian, Heinz (1888–1954)

A Prussian General's son, Guderian was a career soldier who studied tank tactics. He and his troops led the invasion of Poland in 1939. He also led the 2nd Panzer Group in the invasion of Russia in 1941, but after disagreements with his superiors, he was dismissed. Guderian was recalled in March 1943, but in July lost disastrously at the Battle of Kirsk. He became commander of the General Staff in July 1944, but argued with Hitler over military strategy, and was dismissed again. He was captured by US troops in May 1945, but was released in June 1948. He died in 1954.

Heinz Guderian.

'Bomber' Harris.

Harris, Arthur 'Bomber' (1892–1984)

Harris became Commander-in-Chief of RAF Bomber Command in February 1942, and developed the concept of area bombing (blanket bombing). Harris was severely criticized for this tactic, but he argued that the attacks on Hamburg, Cologne and Dresden were intended to break German civilian morale. Indeed, some 600,000 civilians were killed in the raids. He later assisted in the formation of the Pathfinders, an attempt to ease the transition to precision bombing. By the end of the war, nearly 60,000 Bomber Command crew had been lost. In 1946 Harris became Marshal of the Royal Air Force, but retired soon after. He died in April 1984.

Hess, Rudolf (1894–1987)

After the Nazis came to power in 1932, Hess became Deputy Führer. Despite this, he was often left out of the decision-making, and he became more isolated from Hitler. On 10 May 1941 he navigated an aircraft across the North Sea and landed near the home of the Duke of Hamilton in Scotland, whom he had met in 1936. Hess desired to secure peace with Great Britain and presented his captors with a peace proposal; Hitler disowned him and the British dismissed his offers. Hess remained in prison throughout the war, coming to trial at Nuremberg. He was sentenced to life imprisonment, but committed suicide in prison at the age of 92 years.

Rudolf Hess.

Heydrich, Reinhard (1902–42)

Heydrich was a member of the Sicherheitsdienst (SD) – the SS security and intelligence service. Together with Himmler, he was responsible for rounding up Hitler's opponents and became second in command of the Gestapo. After the fall of Poland (1939), Heydrich formed death squads to liquidate leading Polish figures, followed by the two million Jews in Poland. He convened the Warsaw Conference in Berlin in January 1942 to coordinate the extermination of the European Jewish population, but was attacked by Czechoslovakian agents in Prague, dying from blood poisoning a few days later. The Czech village of Lidice was liquidated in reprisal.

Nazi Heinrich Himmler.

Himmler, Heinrich (1900–45)

Himmler was appointed leader of the Schutzstaffel (SS) in 1929. In 1936, he became leader of the Gestapo and four years later established the Waffen SS. Himmler's SS controlled the concentration camps across the occupied lands of Europe and dealt with internal security. Convinced that Germany needed to come to terms with the western Allies or face oblivion, Hitler was informed of Himmler's intentions in April 1945 and ordered his arrest. Himmler disappeared, with an assumed name, but was arrested by the British in Bremen on 22 May. He committed suicide before he could be questioned.

Hitler, Adolf (1889–1945)

By the early 1920s Hitler was involved in right-wing German politics, and in 1923 he attempted a coup and was briefly imprisoned. The Nazi Party became the second largest force in German politics by 1930, gaining the majority by 1932, and in 1933 Hitler became Chancellor. Rounding up opponents, breaking up meetings, crushing the Communists and trade unions, by the end of 1933 150,000 people had been sent to camps. Hitler began regaining German prestige, rejoining with Austria in 1938, seizing Czechoslovakia and then invading Poland in 1939. By the end of 1940, Hitler had humbled the Allies and was ready to turn on Russia. As German troops took territories, Nazi policies of submission and liquidation ravaged Europe. However, Hitler's powers began to decline after the Siege of Stalingrad in 1943; he started suffering from insomnia and spasms, and blaming others for his failures. He committed suicide as the Russians arrived in Germany on 30 April 1945.

German leader Adolf Hitler making a radio broadcast.

Horrocks, Brian (1895–1985)

Horrocks was a career soldier, who by 1939 was in France with Montgomery. During the Dunkirk evacuation he became a Brigadier. After Dunkirk, he took command of defences in the Brighton area in anticipation of the German invasion. When Montgomery took over from Auchinleck in North Africa in 1942, Horrocks joined him, fighting all the way to Tunisia in 1943. Horrocks commanded XXX Corps for the D-Day landings and for Operation Market Garden. He commanded the troops who successfully captured Amiens, Brussels, Antwerp and Bremen between June 1944 and April 1945. After the war Horrocks returned to Britain. He died in 1985.

Brian Horrocks.

Kesselring, Albert (1881–1960)

Kesselring was a member of the Luftwaffe, and in 1936 became Goering's Chief of Staff. He commanded the 1st Air Fleet in the Polish campaign and the 2nd in the invasions of France, Belgium and Holland in 1940. Transferred to the Mediterranean in 1941, he was appointed Deputy Commander of Italian forces in 1942. In 1944 Kesselring was injured in a traffic accident and had to retire. He was captured by the Allies on 6 May 1945, tried and condemned to death. He was granted a reprieve on the grounds of ill-health and released in 1952. He died on 11 July 1960.

Albert Kesselring.

Leclerc, Jacques (1902–47)

French Captain Leclerc was seriously wounded near the River Aube in 1940. He escaped capture and joined de Gaulle's Free French movement. As a major in Cameroon, he took the country from Vichy forces and became Commandant of Chad, launching raids against the Italians in Libya. Leclerc fought as an independent commander under General Montgomery in North Africa, and then moved to Patton's command in France. Leclerc's men were honoured to be the first Allied troops to enter liberated Paris on 25 August 1944, and were involved in the offensives against Germany itself. He was killed in an aircraft crash in 1947.

French military leader Jacques Leclerc.

MacArthur, Douglas (1880–1964)

Douglas MacArthur served as Supreme Commander of the Southwest Pacific Area and, with Admiral Nimitz, planned an offensive against the Japanese that led to the Battles of Midway and the Coral Sea. By early 1944 some 100,000 Japanese had been isolated and MacArthur planned to retake the Philippines. The Battle of Leyte Gulf crippled the Japanese and in March 1945 MacArthur took Manila. MacArthur's last major operation was against Okinawa in April 1945. In 1950 MacArthur took command of UN forces in Korea, but was removed the following year after requesting the use of nuclear weapons against North Korea and China. He died in April 1964.

US commander General Douglas MacArthur.

Mao Tse-tung (1893–1976)

In 1934 Mao became Chairman of the Communist Party and leader of the army, at a time when China was engaged in a bitter civil war with the Kuomitang (Chinese Nationalists). During World War II Mao and Chiang Kai-shek, leader of the Kuomitang, endured an alliance in order to combat the Japanese, but once they had been defeated, China plunged back into civil war, which ultimately saw Mao's Communists gain control of the country. Mao attempted to steer the country through a series of revolutionary changes until 1969. By 1972, however, Mao, desperately ill, was beginning to take a back seat. He died in 1976.

Molotov, Vyacheslav (1890–1986)

As Stalin's Commissar for Foreign Affairs, Molotov signed the German-Russian Pact in 1939. In September 1940, Molotov was warned by the German Foreign Minister, Joachim von Ribbentrop, that Germany was about to join a pact with Italy and Japan. Molotov's spy network had already uncovered this information, and by December 1940 he had received advanced intelligence on the proposed invasion of the Soviet Union. Throughout the war Molotov remained at Stalin's side, attending all the conferences. After the war Molotov was demoted to a post in Mongolia before being expelled from the Communist Party in 1964. He died in Moscow in November 1986.

Russian statesman Vyacheslav Molotov.

Montgomery, Bernard (1887–1976)

British Major-General Montgomery extricated his 2nd Corps from France via Dunkirk in June 1940. In October 1942 he launched Operation Lightfoot, and in November his Operation Supercharge recaptured Tobruk and Tripoli, and forced the Axis surrender in North Africa. He was instrumental in the invasion of Sicily and the Italian mainland in 1943, and in command of all ground troops for D-Day in June 1944. He also masterminded Operation Market Garden in September 1944. In 1945 Montgomery became Commander of the British occupation troops in Germany and later Deputy Supreme Commander of Allied forces in Europe. He died on 25 March 1976.

Mountbatten, Louis (1900–79)

Lord Louis Mountbatten was a career naval officer and the great-grandson of Queen Victoria. In 1941 he was appointed Head of Combined Operations command; he organized a number of commando raids, notably the Dieppe Raid in August 1942. Mountbatten assumed command of South-East Asia Command (SEAC) in October 1943, charged with dealing with the Japanese in Singapore and Burma. After the war Mountbatten, as Viceroy of India, steered India and Pakistan towards independence. He later commanded the Mediterranean fleet, served four years as First Sea Lord and then served as Chief of Defence staff. He was killed on 27 August 1979, a victim of Irish terrorism.

Mussolini, Benito (1883–1945)

Italian leader Benito Mussolini.

Mussolini organized right-wing groups in Italy's Fascist Party before rising to power in 1922. By 1929 Italy had become a one-party state; Mussolini was popular, carrying out reforms and public works programmes. In 1939 he signed a military alliance with Germany and Italy entered the war in June 1940, fighting in North Africa and Egypt. However, they were dependent on Germany by late 1941.

Mussolini's position was undermined after the fall of Sicily in July 1943, and he was arrested. Freed in September – on orders from Hitler – he set up a rival government in Northern Italy. By 1944, German resistance in Italy was crumbling, Rome fell on 4 June followed by Florence on 12 August. When the British 8th Army crossed the River Po on 23 April 1945, Mussolini and his mistress attempted to flee. They were captured on 27 April 1945; they were shot in Milan and their bodies displayed as a warning to others.

Chester Nimitz.

Nimitz, Chester (1885–1966)

Nimitz was a career US naval officer and expert on submarine warfare. After Pearl Harbor, assigned to the Pacific Fleet, he took offensive actions against the Marshall and Gilbert Islands. Nimitz was instrumental in causing the defeat of the Japanese navy in the Coral Sea and Midway. He worked with Douglas MacArthur and King (Commander-in-Chief of the US Fleet), finding himself between these two leaders' differing opinions of how the Pacific War should be fought. Appointed Fleet Admiral in December 1944, he ultimately replaced King in November 1945. Nimitz retired in 1947, and became a functionary of the United Nations. He died on 20 February 1966.

Patton, George (1885–1945)

Patton was a controversial US military commander. By the time of the Sicily landings, he was commanding the 7th Army, taking Palermo and cutting off 50,000 Italian troops. He was implicated in the murder of over 70 Italian prisoners of war, and was replaced in January 1944. By August he was back in command in France, staging the Allied breakout that reached the River Meuse. Patton's troops destroyed German resistance after their failed Ardennes offensive in December 1944 and his troops crossed the Rhine on 22 March 1945. Patton was briefly made Governor of Bavaria before being removed from office. He died on 21 December 1945.

US general George Patton.

Peiper, Joachim (1915–76)

Joachim Peiper.

Peiper joined the Hitler Youth in 1933, entering the SS the following year. At the time of the Ardennes offensive he was a Lieutenant Colonel and spearheaded the offensive. He managed to make the best progress in the entire campaign, covering 100 km (62 miles) in 72 hours. He was captured and put on trial at Dachau, where he took full responsibility for what he had done, including the alleged massacre at Malmedy. Nonetheless, he was not sentenced to death and was released in 1956. He died in a house fire on 13 July 1976 – possibly the victim of an arson attack.

Pétain, Henri-Phillipe (1856–1951)

Field Marshal Pétain was appointed War Minister of France in 1934. He agreed to serve as the Chief of State of Vichy France after the surrender of France in 1940. Pétain signed an armistice with Germany and agreed to administer roughly 20 per cent of France, which would remain unoccupied by the Germans. He agreed to deport all Jews, maintain an army of 100,000 and actively prevent Frenchmen from joining the Allies. Vichy troops, under Pétain's orders, resisted Allied actions in the Middle East and North Africa, but after the D-Day landings in June 1944 Pétain fled to Switzerland.

Quisling, Vidkun (1887–1945)

Quisling was leader of the Norwegian Nasjonal Samling Party, a pro-German fascist group. When Germany invaded Norway, Quisling fully supported the action. In 1942 the German Reichskommisor of Norway, Josef Terboven, named Quisling Minister President (Prime Minister), a post he assumed on 1 February 1943. Although his relationship with Terboven was difficult, Quisling avidly followed German instructions and policies throughout the war. After Germany's surrender, Quisling faced charges of treason. He was found guilty and was executed by firing squad on 24 October 1945.

Norwegian fascist Vidkun Quisling, who supported the German invasion.

Joachim von Ribbentrop.

Ribbentrop, Joachim von (1893–1946)

Ribbentrop joined the Nazi Party in May 1932 and became Hitler's foreign affairs advisor. He was appointed Ambassador to London in 1936 and Foreign Minister in 1938. He was involved in negotiations with the British and French during the late 1930s and the German-Soviet Pact of 1939. Ribbentrop faded into the background during the remainder of the war, yet the Allies were convinced he was implicated in German racial policies and war crimes. He was tried and convicted at Nuremberg, and sentenced to death; his execution was carried out on 16 October 1946.

Rommel, Erwin (1891–1944)

Rommel commanded Germany's 7th Panzer Division and planned the campaign against the western nations, launching the invasion and reaching Cherbourg on 19 June 1940. In February 1941, he commanded the Deutsches Afrika Korps in Tripoli and swept across North Africa on the offensive. The Allies launched their offensive in October, and pursued the 'Desert Fox' back across North Africa. Transferred to France in December 1943, Rommel was injured in an aircraft attack on 17 July 1944. Three days later – implicated in the plot to assassinate Hitler – he was given the choice of suicide or execution as a traitor; he chose suicide.

Erwin Rommel.

Roosevelt, Franklin D. (1882–1945)

Roosevelt became President of the United States in November 1932, serving the first of four terms. The US was in the middle of the Depression at the time, with 13 million people unemployed. In the first few days of his presidency, Roosevelt enacted a sweeping recovery programme, which turned the country around. He adopted an isolationist policy but was firmly and implacably opposed to the Nazi regime and the intentions of Japan. However, after the attack on Pearl Harbor Roosevelt mobilized the United States into an irresistible fighting machine. He died before he could see the fruits of his victories, on 12 April 1945.

US President Franklin D. Roosevelt.

Slim, William (1897–1970)

British commander William Slim fought in the Sudan, Abyssinia and Eritrea then in the Middle East until he was transferred to Burma in March 1942. Slim's summer 1943 offensive to capture Akyab ended in failure and he was ultimately succeeded by Mountbatten. In March 1944 he successfully defended Assam from the Japanese and participated in the offensive later that year, taking Mandalay in March 1945. His defence led to the British capture of Rangoon in May 1945. After the war Slim became the Head of the Imperial Defence College before succeeding Montgomery as Chief of the Imperial Staff. He died in December 1970.

Stalin, Joseph (1879–1953)

Stalin became leader of Russia's Communist Party by ordering the murder of all other leading figures associated with the Russian Revolution. He maintained his grip by mass arrests, death sentences and exile in Siberian labour camps during a succession of purges. In 1937 he began a series of purges in the Red Army, which liquidated nearly all higher ranking officers. In 1939 he signed a non-aggression pact with Hitler, agreeing their spheres of influence in Eastern Europe, including the division of Poland. His invasion of Finland proved disastrous and when the Germans launched Operation Barbarossa (June 1941), the incompetence of the Red Army allowed the Germans to overrun Western Russia. The entry of the United States in late 1941 provided the Russians with much-needed war material, but it was his commander Zhukov that ultimately saved Russia. Stalin remained in place after the war and moulded much of Eastern Europe in his vision of a Communist state.

Stilwell, Joseph (1883–1946)

In February 1942 Stilwell was put in command of US forces in China, Burma and India before being appointed Deputy Supreme Allied Commander under Mountbatten in August 1943. He launched an offensive against Japanese-held Burma and assumed the role of Personnel Commander of Operations in December 1943. But when the Japanese launched their Ichi-Go offensive in China in 1944, overrunning US airfields in China, Stilwell was recalled to the US. He returned to active duty in order to clean up Japanese resistance in Okinawa (June 1945), and briefly took over as Governor of Okinawa before being recalled to Washington. Stilwell died on 12 October 1946.

US military leader Joseph Stilwell.

Tito, Josip (1892–1981)

After the German invasion of Yugoslavia, Communist revolutionary Josip Tito helped set up Partisan units to fight the Germans. Tito ably led the Partisans in their bloody struggle and in November 1943 he established a government in Bosnia. A new Yugoslavian government was established under Ivan Subasic in May 1944; Tito served as War Minister, but continued to lead his Partisans until they had liberated Belgrade. Tito became the Premier of Yugoslavia in March 1945 and created a new Federal Republic. After the war he broke with Russia and pursued his own policies for Yugoslavia. He died on 4 May 1981.

Tojo, Hideki (1884–1948)

One of the principal architects of Japanese involvement in the war, Tojo served as Vice Minister of War before becoming commander of the air forces. Tojo had supported an aggressive foreign policy, arguing that pre-emptive attacks on China and Russia were the only way to ensure Japan's long-term prospects. It was Tojo who ordered the attack on Pearl Harbor on 7 December 1941, when a negotiated settlement with the US seemed doomed to failure. After the war he was captured by US forces, tried as a war criminal, found guilty and executed on 23 December 1948.

Wavell, Archibald (1883–1950)

As commander of British army forces in the Middle East, Wavell faced Italy's attempt to capture Egypt in 1939. He successfully pushed the Italians back, but by March 1941 Wavell faced Rommel, who forced the British out of Libya. Wavell was then sent to Burma, where he unsuccessfully attempted to force out the Japanese. He became the Viceroy of Burma and was later replaced by Lord Mountbatten. Wavell returned to England in 1947 and became Lord Lieutenant of the County of London. He died in May 1950.

Wingate's guerrillas.

Wingate, Orde (1903–44)

Wingate was a British career soldier. In 1939 he was sent to command Gideon Force in the Sudan and led successful attacks on Italian-held Abyssinia. He was then posted to India, where he formed the Chindits. Wingate's major offensive began on 14 March

1944, with the Chindits operating 322 km (200 miles) behind Japanese lines. Wingate's men caused immense damage to the Japanese throughout Burma. Losses were high and Wingate himself died when his aircraft went down near Imphal on 14 March 1944.

Yamamoto, Isokoru (1884–1943)

Yamamoto became the Minister of the Japanese Navy in 1938 and proposed the plan to make a pre-emptive strike on the US fleet at Pearl Harbor in 1941. He organized the invasions of the Solomon Islands and New Guinea, and in the summer of 1942 he attempted to capture Midway Island. The attack was an unmitigated disaster. His attempts to prevent the US from taking Guadalcanal (November 1942) also failed. Yamamoto was killed during Operation Vengeance, in which US aircraft shot down his transport over Bougainville on 18 April 1943. His death was not officially reported by the Japanese until 21 May.

Yamashita, Tomoyuki (1888–1946)

As commander of the Japanese 25th Army, Yamashita outmanoeuvred the British in Malaya and Singapore in 1942. In February 1943 he was promoted to General and placed in command of the Philippines. He attempted to form independent guerrilla units to resist the US invasion, but was captured by US troops on 2 September 1945. He was found guilty of alleged Japanese atrocities on the Philippines during the war and hanged on 23 February 1946.

Zhukov, Georgy (1896–1974)

Russian soldier Zhukov joined the Communists in 1917. Interested in armoured warfare, his knowledge convinced Stalin to appoint him Chief of Staff in 1940. Zhukov, unable to prevent the slaughter and surrender of Russian troops in the early years, saved Moscow. He rebuilt the army and transformed the machines that fought to Hitler's door.

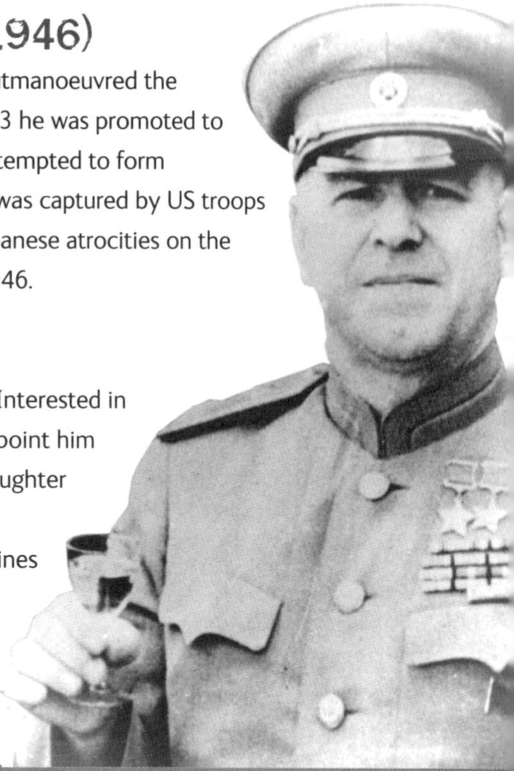

Georgy Zhukov

THE POST-WAR LEGACY

A COMPLEX LEGACY

The peace of 1945 had sought to settle many of the issues that had been the root cause of war in 1939. In reality, however, the end of World War II posed more questions and potential problems than it had resolved.

The French Problem

One of the first major problems was the loss of power and prestige for the French. They had for a period of time lost the ability to control their empire and what was more, their empire in the Far East had suffered enormously during Japanese occupation. This would leave a smouldering ember that would eventually spark the Vietnam War.

The Iron Curtain Comes Down

In Europe, no sooner had the Potsdam Conference broken up than the shutters came down, pitting East against West for 40 years. It was only after the economic collapse of the Soviet Union, long after the death of Stalin, that many countries in Eastern Europe could once again move towards democracy.

Broken Britain

The impact on Britain was perhaps the most severe. Although it had not been occupied by Germany, its far-flung possessions had either been menaced or taken during the six years of the war. Economically the country was ruined, owing billions to its banker, the United States. Whilst many European countries enjoyed the benefits of post-war programmes to rebuild what had been destroyed during the war, it was notable that Britain, as a victor, received little or none of this assistance.

The D–Day landings in June 1944.

Long-Lasting Legacies

At least two more legacies remained to haunt the world. The state of Yugoslavia, which had fought amongst itself as much as against its occupiers during the war, did not last much beyond the death of Tito. Each formerly independent state splintered down ethnic lines, causing death and destruction on a scale not seen in Europe since the war itself. Most recently the post-war legacy has brought two separate conflicts to the Middle East. In reparation for the suffering of Jews in Europe, many nations supported the creation of the state of Israel, which has been at loggerheads with its neighbours since the 1940s. Equally, in

St Paul's survived for future generations to admire.

Iraq – a country whose borders were determined primarily by the British – ethnic differences led to the domination of one group over another for several decades before finally, in 2003, two long-term allies, Britain and the US had to step in and deal with the issue.

Great Losses

There have been various estimates of the number of deaths directly attributed to World War II. Conservatively, the total can be put at just over 56 million worldwide. Russia and China suffered worst, with 21.3 million and 11.3 million respectively. Germany had lost just over seven million, a similar number to Poland. Even countries whose territory was never threatened to any great degree, such as Australia, New Zealand, South Africa and Canada, all lost tens of thousands.

Beyond Living Memory

As 1939 is more than 70 years since the present day, there are precious few World War II veterans left alive. Only the youngest, or those who experienced the final few years of the war now remain. Their dwindling numbers have not diminished the pride and the sorrow of remembrance. True history, it has been said, applies only to times that are sufficiently distant in the memory, and where none remain who personally experienced that age. All too soon the veterans who personally experienced World War II will also be gone.

Global Conflict

Without doubt World War II represented a truly global conflict in a far more significant and all-encompassing manner than any other conflict before it. Although World War I had seen horrendous carnage on the Western Front and in the East, elsewhere in the world the conflict had been restricted to a handful of other locations. In World War II even the most remote and strategically protected countries were not immune to attack. Of the major belligerents in the war, only the US did not suffer any domestic losses as a result of action on the home front.

An Indelible Scar?

People can be forgiven for assuming that the principle victims of World War II were the Jews, who were slaughtered in their millions by the Germans in those years. There are no words to describe the horror of genocide, nor the systematic and cold-hearted way in which the Germans carried out the task. While the key figures in the Nazi regime paid for their decisions and their politics, either at Nuremberg or by their own hands, there were thousands of others who left indelible scars, not just on the victims themselves and their families, but their ancestors several generations removed.

The war's lasting legacy is the fact that after several generations, those across the world who are far too young to remember any of the direct consequences of World War II, remain fascinated and engaged by the collective memory of it.

RESOURCES

Further Reading

Ambrose, Stephen E., *D-Day, June 6 1944 – The Battle for the Normandy Beaches*, Pocket Books, 2002

Atkinson, Rick, *An Army at Dawn: The War in North Africa 1942–1943*, Little, Brown, 2003

Beevor, Antony, *Stalingrad*, Penguin, 1999

Beevor, Antony, *The Fall of Berlin 1945*, Penguin, 2003

Bullock, Alan, *Hitler and Stalin: Parallel Lives*, Fontana Press, 1998

Calvocoressi, Peter, *World Politics Since 1945*, New York, 1991

Calvocoressi, Peter, et al, *The Penguin History of the Second World War*, Penguin, 2003

Chandler, David, *The Dictionary of Battles*, London, 1987

Churchill, Winston, *The Second World War*, Pimlico, 2002

Gilbert, Martin, *Second World War*, Phoenix, 2009

Gilbert, Martin, *The Holocaust*, HarperCollins, 1987

Gilbert, Martin, *Churchill: A Life*, Pimlico, 2000

Hart, L., *The History of the Second World War*, London, 1970

Holland, James, *Fortress Malta: An Island Under Siege 1940–1943*, Orion, 2003

Jackson, Julian, *France: The Dark Years, 1940–1944*, Oxford University Press, 2003

Jackson, Julian, *The Fall of France: The Nazi Invasion of 1940*, Oxford University Press, 2003

Kershaw, Ian, *Hitler 1936–1945*, Penguin, 2001

Layton, Geoff, *Germany: The Third Reich 1933–45*, Hodder and Stoughton, 2000

Messenger, Charles, *The Century of Warfare: Worldwide Conflict from 1900 to the Present Day*, London, 1995

Morgan, Kenneth O. (ed.), *The Oxford Illustrated History of Britain*, Oxford, 1997

Ryan, Cornelius, *A Bridge Too Far*, Wordsworth Editions, 1999

Sweeman, John, *et al.*, *The Dambusters*, Time Warner, 2003

Trotter, William R., *The Winter War: The Russo-Finnish War of 1939–40*, Aurum Books, 2002

Weintraub, Stanley, *Long Day's Journey Into War: December 7 1941*, Lyons Press, 2001

Young, Peter (ed), *The Cassell Atlas of the Second World War*, Cassell, 1999

Websites

www.bbc.co.uk/history/worldwars/wwtwo
www.ibiblio.org/hyperwar
www.codesandciphers.org.uk/
www.spartacus.schoolnet.co.uk/2WW.htm

INDEX

Page numbers in **bold** refer to main entries